MW01484853

EXIT READY

ROCKS, ROLES, AND RESULTS
THAT POWER YOUR EXIT PLAN

EXIT READY

ROCKS, ROLES, AND RESULTS
THAT POWER YOUR EXIT PLAN

Tyler Smith with Kelly J. Carter

Foreword and Bonus Chapter by
Gino Wickman
Author of *Traction* & *Shine*
Creator of EOS®

Printed in the United States of America

Published by Igniting Souls
PO Box 43, Powell, OH 43065
IgnitingSouls.com

LCCN: 2025916048
Paperback ISBN: 978-1-63680-555-9
Hardcover ISBN: 978-1-63680-556-6
e-book ISBN: 978-1-63680-557-3

Available in paperback, hardcover, e-book, and audiobook.

Any Internet addresses (websites, blogs, etc.) and telephone numbers printed in this book are offered as a resource. They are not intended in any way to be or imply an endorsement by Igniting Souls, nor does Igniting Souls vouch for the content of these sites and numbers for the life of this book.

Some names and identifying details may have been changed to protect the privacy of individuals.

EOS®, The Entrepreneurial Operating System®, Traction®, and EOS Implementer® are registered trademarks owned by EOS Worldwide, LLC. For a complete list of trademarks owned by EOS Worldwide throughout this book, please visit branding.eosworldwide.com/eos-trademarks/.

Boat Drinks & Banana Jumpers

CONTENTS

PART 3: EXIT READY PROCESS

FOREWORD BY GINO WICKMAN

Let me begin by saying something you might not expect from someone who's lived the entire entrepreneurial journey from startup to exit. Selling your company is scary, hard, overwhelming, stressful, and deeply emotional. If you feel that way right now, you're not alone…I've been there too.

The first company I sold, I did it all wrong. I didn't find the right buyer. I didn't negotiate the best deal. I wasn't ready emotionally. I didn't have the right team around me. And worst of all, I didn't have a clear plan. I paid for it. It haunted me.

The second company I sold, I did it right. I took everything I learned from the first experience and flipped the script. I slowed down. I chose the right team to support me. I got aligned. I stayed in control. I created an exit that felt great. It was clean, strong, and intentional. I walked away proud of how I handled it and excited for what was next.

I want you to avoid the pain of a bad exit and experience the clarity of a great one.

What you're holding in your hands is the exact process I wish I had when I sold the first time. *Exit Ready* takes out the guesswork. It gives you the structure, tools, and guidance to make one of the biggest decisions of your life without losing yourself in the process.

If you run on EOS and plan to exit, this book is a natural fit. Once you've built a strong leadership team and implemented the EOS tools, the next step is to become Exit-Ready. The Step-by-Step Exit (SxSE) system picks up once EOS is implemented and the company is living in the 90-Day World®. It walks you through every phase of exit-readiness and planning.

SxSE doesn't just deal with the external. It also addresses what most founders and owners ignore until it's too late: your inner world.

That's where "The 10 Disciplines" come in. Tyler and I decided they are a perfect fit for those considering an exit. I'm presenting them in this book in their abbreviated form.

In my book *Shine*, co-authored with Rob Dube, we lay out ten powerful disciplines that help driven people like you create space, energy, and peace while still achieving big results. They will help you know your boundaries in an exit, as well as in life. These are not fluff. They are battle-tested disciplines I use in my own life every day and through my second exit. Things like "Know Thyself," "Be Still," "10-Year Thinking," and "Say No…Often." When you install these disciplines, you stop reacting and start responding. You lead from a place of clarity instead of fear.

And during a high-stakes exit, that clarity is everything.

The SxSE Model even recommends a seat at the table for a Personal Coach, the person or resource responsible for helping you navigate the emotional journey. For many, *The 10 Disciplines* becomes that coach. They are your compass when the road gets bumpy.

This book isn't about rushing to a finish line. It's about helping you make the most important transition of your life with strength, calm, and confidence.

You've worked hard to build your company. You deserve to leave on your terms, without regret. Read this book. Follow the process. Use the tools. Tap into the disciplines. Get focused to move forward with peace of mind.

Here's to your next great adventure... planned with precision, anchored in peace, and executed on your terms.

—Gino Wickman
Author of *Traction* & *Shine*,
Creator of EOS®

INTRODUCTION: ARE YOU TRULY READY?

So, you've built a business. Not just any business, but one that you've poured your heart, soul, time, and hard-earned money into. You discovered the power of the Entrepreneurial Operating System®, EOS®, and embraced its disciplines. Your company is likely running better than it ever has. You've got a Vision, clear as day, shared by everyone. The right people are in the right seats, excelling in their roles. You have a firm grip on your numbers, understanding the story they tell. Your team tackles issues head-on, solving them for the long term. Your core processes are documented, creating consistency and scalability. And most importantly, you've got real, measurable Traction®. You're moving forward, achieving your goals. That's a monumental achievement, and you should be proud.

But even with all that success, a question probably nags at you, perhaps in the quiet hours of the night: *What happens when it's time to step away?* What's the next chapter for you, and for the business you've painstakingly built?

Every single business owner, without exception, will exit their business someday. It's an unavoidable truth. That exit might be a carefully orchestrated event, the culmination of years of planning. Or, it could be thrust upon you unexpectedly, a sudden turn forced by circumstances beyond your control. We call these the "5 Ds": Disability, Death, Disagreement, Divorce, or Distress. Any one of these can trigger an unplanned, often chaotic, departure. And if you're caught unprepared, the fall-out can be devastating. Not just for you and your financial future, but for your family who depends on you, for your loyal employees who've helped build your dream, for your customers who rely on your products or services, and for the very legacy you've worked so hard to create.

This is precisely why achieving Exit Readiness is not just important, it's absolutely essential. And here's a critical distinction: Exit Readiness isn't merely about prepping for a far-off sale that might happen someday. It's about cultivating a stronger, more resilient, more marketable, and ultimately more valuable business *today*, every single day. This book is your guide to that transformation. We're here to introduce you to the Step-by-Step Exit (SxSE) system, a methodology meticulously designed for businesses like yours—businesses that are already leveraging the power of EOS—to help you achieve a state of perpetual Exit Readiness.

Our promise is to show you, in clear, actionable terms, how to elevate your already well-run EOS company into an organization that's primed for a smooth, successful, and highly profitable transition, whenever that time may come. The SxSE system isn't a replacement for EOS; it's a natural and powerful extension of it. It seamlessly integrates with the EOS framework you know and trust, layering in the critical perspectives and preparations needed for an optimal exit. A core part of this is the Six1 Framework—your single, unifying operating system (EOS) harmonized with six indispensable trusted advisors. Together, they form a complete, holistic approach to mastering your exit.

But before we delve into the mechanics of the SxSE system, let's consider the real-world implications through the contrasting experiences of two business owners. Their stories paint a vivid picture of why this matters so profoundly.

A TALE OF TWO EXITS

David and Sarah were smart, driven entrepreneurs who had successfully built their respective companies into thriving $10 million enterprises, both diligently applying the principles of EOS. After two decades of dedication, they each decided it was time to sell and move on to their next adventures.

David, confident in his company's profitability and smooth operations, assumed that selling would be a straightforward process. He engaged a business broker, listed his company, and waited for the offers to flood in. He believed his well-run EOS company was inherently sellable at a premium. However, the due diligence process, that intense scrutiny by potential buyers, quickly unearthed a series of significant problems.

Buyers discovered that David, despite his best intentions, was still the central cog in the machine. Nearly every major decision flowed through him. Critical customer relationships were almost entirely dependent on his personal involvement. The company's financial reporting, while adequate for internal use, wasn't up to the rigorous standards expected by sophisticated buyers. Perhaps most critically, his management team, while competent, lacked the demonstrated ability to operate the business autonomously without his constant guidance. To compound matters, several unaddressed legal and tax issues emerged, casting shadows of doubt and increasing perceived risk.

The result? Months of frustrating negotiations, dwindling buyer interest, and mounting stress. David eventually accepted an offer that was substantially below his initial expectations, and it came with a demanding three-year earnout provision. This meant he was tied to the business, working harder than ever, just to hopefully realize the full, diminished value of his sale. Within a year, key employees, sensing instability and a lack of future opportunity, began to leave. Some important customers, unsettled by the changes and the departure of familiar faces, defected to competitors. David's dream of a smooth exit had morphed into a prolonged, exhausting ordeal.

Sarah, on the other hand, approached her exit with a different mindset and a proactive strategy. Three years before her intended departure, she made a crucial decision: She engaged a specialist exit planning advisor and began to implement the principles of what we now call the Step-by-Step Exit (SxSE) system. One of her first actions was to assemble her Six1 team of trusted advisors—legal, financial, tax, M&A, wealth, and a personal coach—ensuring they worked in concert towards her exit goals.

Systematically, Sarah worked to reduce her day-to-day operational involvement. She meticulously transferred critical knowledge and key relationships from herself to her empowered leadership team. Sarah invested in cleaning up her financial reporting, ensuring it was transparent, accurate, and presented in a buyer-friendly format, and implemented systems to track the key performance indicators and value drivers that sophisticated buyers scrutinize. Proactively, with her advisory team, she identified and addressed potential legal and tax issues long before they could become deal-breakers. Crucially, she focused on building a robust, cohesive leadership team that was demonstrably capable of running and growing the business independently of her.

When Sarah finally decided it was time to sell, her M&A advisor orchestrated a controlled, competitive auction process that attracted multiple qualified and enthusiastic buyers. The due diligence phase was remarkably smooth because Sarah was thoroughly prepared; there were no surprises, no hidden skeletons. Several offers exceeded her target valuation, giving her significant leverage, which allowed her to negotiate highly favorable terms, including a clean break with minimal post-closing obligations. The entire sale process, from accepting an offer to closing the deal, was completed within an impressive 120 days.

Sarah walked away from her business with significantly more money in her pocket than David, despite their businesses being comparable in size and profitability. More importantly, she walked away with her peace of mind intact. Years later, she was thoroughly enjoying her next chapter, secure in the knowledge that

> **EXIT READINESS IS NOT A SINGULAR EVENT YOU SCRAMBLE FOR AT THE LAST MINUTE.**

the business she built continued to thrive under its new ownership. David, meanwhile, was still mired in the complexities of his earnout, his exit far from the liberating experience he had envisioned.

The chasm between David's and Sarah's outcomes wasn't a matter of luck or circumstance. It was a direct result of preparation—or the critical lack of it. Sarah understood a fundamental truth that often eludes many entrepreneurs:

> Exit readiness is not a singular event
> you scramble for at the last minute.

It is a deliberate, strategic process. She embraced a systematic approach to preparing her business for its ultimate transition, and the rewards were undeniable. This book is dedicated to helping you become like Sarah, to equip you with the knowledge and tools to navigate your own exit with foresight, strategy, and confidence.

WHY EXIT READINESS MATTERS MORE THAN EVER

You might be thinking, *This is interesting, but I'm not planning to sell my business anytime soon. Why should I divert my attention to exit readiness now?* It's a fair question, and the answer is multifaceted and compelling. Exit Readiness transcends the mere act of selling; it's about fundamentally building a better, stronger, more resilient, and ultimately more valuable business *today*, while simultaneously securing your options and freedom for tomorrow.

> *Being Exit Ready goes beyond knowing what your business is worth—it's about developing a strategic plan now to preserve that value. The right exit strategy safeguards not only your financial outcome but the legacy you've built for your family—ensuring wealth isn't lost to taxes, missteps, or missed opportunities.*
>
> —Kelly J. Carter, CEO BRPG

Consider the immediate, tangible benefits that accrue when your business is perpetually Exit-Ready:

First, you achieve **Higher Business Value**. The very factors that make your business appealing and less risky to a potential buyer—strong leadership, clean financials, documented processes, diversified customer base, reduced owner dependence—are the same factors that enhance its intrinsic value and profitability in the present moment. An Exit-Ready business is simply a more valuable asset, period.

Second, you gain **More Personal Freedom**. As your business becomes less dependent on your daily involvement, you reclaim your time and energy. You can choose to focus on higher-level strategic initiatives, explore new ventures, or simply take that extended vacation you've been dreaming about for years, confident that the business will continue to operate smoothly in your absence.

Third, you experience **Reduced Risk**. Life is unpredictable. The 5 Ds we mentioned earlier—Disability, Death, Disagreement, Divorce, Distress—can strike at any time. Being Exit-Ready means you've proactively mitigated many of the risks associated with such unforeseen events, protecting not only your financial interests but also the well-being of your family, your employees, and the continuity of the business itself.

Fourth, you enjoy **Better Sleep and Peace of Mind**. There's an immense sense of security that comes from knowing your business is in top shape, that it could be sold efficiently and for maximum value if the need or desire arose. This peace of mind is invaluable, reducing stress and allowing you to lead with greater clarity and confidence.

> *Exit readiness isn't just about planning for the ideal sale— it's about protecting your business and your family from the unexpected. The 5 D's (Death, Disability, Divorce, Disagreement, and Distress) can force an unplanned exit at any moment, and only a well-prepared owner can navigate those events without losing value, control, or legacy.*
>
> —Kelly J. Carter. CEO BRPG

Fifth, you create **More Options for Your Future**. When your business is Exit-Ready, you're in the driver's seat:

- **Sell to a strategic buyer:** Capture a premium by transferring ownership to a company that values your market position or capabilities.

- **Transition to family or key employees:** Preserve your legacy and reward your team by passing the reins to those who know the business best.

- **Bring in private-equity partners:** Infuse new capital and expertise to accelerate growth, then plan an eventual full exit when value peaks.

- **Step back as a passive owner:** Retain equity, enjoy ongoing returns, and free yourself from day-to-day operations.

- **Opt for a majority recap:** Take a large payout now with outside investors, then keep growing together for a second bite of the apple later.

Exit Readiness is about creating options, not limiting them.

And finally, the discipline inherent in becoming Exit-Ready inevitably drives stronger overall business performance. The focus on systems, accountability, and value creation permeates every aspect of your operations, leading to improved efficiency, enhanced customer satisfaction, and a more engaged and motivated team.

In essence, embracing the journey to Exit Readiness is the logical and strategic next step for any well-run EOS business. There is simply no downside to being better prepared, more valuable, and in greater control of your destiny.

THE EOS ADVANTAGE

If your business is already running on EOS, you possess a significant and undeniable advantage on the path to Exit Readiness. You've already laid a robust foundation by implementing many of the core elements that potential buyers actively seek and highly value.

Your **Clear Vision**, articulated through your Vision/Traction Organizer® (V/TO®), provides essential strategic clarity and direction. Everyone in your organization understands where the company is going and how it plans to get there. This alignment is gold to a buyer.

Your commitment to **Strong Leadership**, fostered through tools like The Accountability Chart® and a focus on the People Component® (Right People, Right Seats), ensures organizational clarity, capability, and accountability. Buyers look for strong management teams that can carry the business forward.

Your use of **Performance Metrics**, tracked via the EOS Scorecard and other Data Component® tools, offers crucial visibility into the operational and financial health of your business. This transparency builds trust and allows buyers to quickly assess performance.

Your developed **Problem-Solving** capabilities, honed through mastering the Issues Component® (Identify, Discuss, Solve—IDS®), create a culture of resilience and continuous improvement. Buyers value businesses that can effectively navigate challenges.

Your **Documented Processes**, a key outcome of strengthening the Process Component® (documenting your core processes and ensuring they are followed by all), enable consistency, scalability, and operational efficiency. This reduces operational risk and makes the business easier to integrate.

And your **Execution Discipline**, driven by the relentless focus of the Traction Component® (Rocks, The Meeting Pulse®, and accountability), ensures that your company consistently achieves its goals. Buyers want businesses that can deliver results.

These foundational elements of EOS are incredibly powerful and provide a tremendous head start. However, it's crucial to recognize that while EOS makes your business well-run, it doesn't automatically make it Exit-Ready. True Exit Readiness requires an additional layer of focus, a specific set of preparations that go beyond day-to-day operational excellence. You need to consciously extend the principles of EOS to address the unique demands and perspectives of the exit process and the buyer's lens.

INTRODUCING THE SXSE SYSTEM: THE EOS-ALIGNED PATH TO EXIT READINESS

The SxSE system is engineered with a singular purpose: to guide EOS companies like yours to a state of complete and perpetual Exit Readiness. It's not a foreign concept you need to learn from scratch; rather, it builds directly upon and integrates seamlessly with the EOS foundation you've already established.

The SxSE system is comprised of four interconnected and indispensable parts:

First, the **SxSE Model**. This provides a clear visual framework that illustrates precisely how EOS and Exit Readiness principles integrate and reinforce each other. It shows you how to layer exit-focused thinking onto each of the Six Key Components® of EOS.

Second, the **Six1 Framework**. This offers a structured and proven approach to coordinating your efforts with your six essential trusted advisors: your legal counsel, financial advisor, tax specialist, M&A (transaction) advisor, wealth manager, and personal coach. Effective collaboration with this team is critical for a successful exit.

Third, the **SxSE Process**. This outlines the clear, step-by-step methodology you will follow to systematically assess your current state of readiness, identify gaps, and implement the necessary changes to become truly Exit-Ready.

Fourth, the **SxSE Toolbox**. This contains a suite of practical, actionable tools and exercises specifically designed to help you implement every aspect of the SxSE system effectively and efficiently.

Throughout this book, we will unpack each of these four parts in detail. We will guide you through assessing your current state of Exit Readiness, developing a comprehensive plan, and systematically addressing the key factors that drive both business value and your ultimate exit options. By the end, you'll possess a clear, actionable roadmap for transforming your well-run EOS business into a truly Exit-Ready enterprise—one that not only maximizes your financial return but also gives you more value, more freedom, and more options, both now and in the future.

So, let's embark on this journey. In Chapter 1, we'll lay the groundwork by exploring the SxSE Model in detail, showing you how it builds upon your existing EOS foundation to create a comprehensive framework for achieving true Exit Readiness.

PART 1

Step-by-Step Model

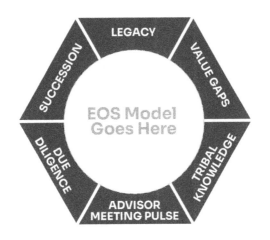

1

THE SXSE MODEL—BUILDING YOUR EXIT-READY SUPERSTRUCTURE

As a dedicated leader running your company on the Entrepreneurial Operating System, you've already constructed a formidable operational foundation. The Six Key Components of EOS—Vision, People, Data, Issues, Process, and Traction—have provided you with a comprehensive and proven framework for running your business with clarity, discipline, and accountability. You've invested the effort, embraced the tools, and your business is undoubtedly stronger, more focused, and more effective as a result. This is the bedrock upon which true Exit Readiness is built.

However, it's a crucial realization for every EOS-run company that a well-oiled operational machine, while essential, isn't automatically primed for a successful, high-value exit. Achieving that requires an additional, deliberate layer of preparation—a superstructure, if you will—specifically designed to maximize your company's attractiveness to potential buyers and ensure a smooth, profitable transition when you decide it's time to move on. This is precisely where the SxSE Model enters the picture. It doesn't seek to replace or reinvent your existing

EOS framework; rather, it builds directly upon it, extending its power and focus towards the unique demands of an exit.

Think of it in these terms: EOS empowers you to build an exceptional, high-performing business. The SxSE Model then takes that exceptional business and meticulously prepares it to be sold, at any time, for its maximum potential value, and on your terms. SxSE is the essential bridge between running a great company today and realizing its full worth tomorrow. It achieves this by embedding specific, exit-focused considerations and actions into each of the Six Key Components you have already mastered.

The synergy is powerful: EOS, combined with SxSE, translates into a business that not only operates with peak efficiency and effectiveness in the present but also systematically builds transferable, marketable value for the future. Many otherwise successful businesses stumble, or even fail, during an attempted exit because their focus remains solely on internal operations, neglecting the critical external perspectives and preparations that buyers demand.

> **THE SXSE MODEL IS ABOUT MOVING FROM A POSITION OF HOPE TO ONE OF STRENGTH.**

The SxSE Model, at its core, is about transforming your business from one that is merely "sellable" into one that is truly "Exit-Ready." This distinction is profound. A sellable business might eventually find a buyer, perhaps after a lengthy process and significant compromises. An Exit-Ready business, on the other hand, commands attention, attracts multiple interested parties, and gives you, the owner, the leverage to dictate favorable terms. It's about moving from a position of hope to one of strength.

One of the most significant transformations the SxSE Model drives is the systematic reduction of owner dependence.

This is often the single biggest hurdle to a successful and lucrative exit. If the business revolves too heavily around you—your knowledge, your relationships, your decision-making—potential buyers see what they term "key person risk." This perceived risk can dramatically diminish your company's valuation, complicate the deal structure (often leading to lengthy and onerous earn-outs), or, in some cases, render the business virtually unsellable at any reasonable price.

The journey from an owner-dependent entity to an owner-independent enterprise is not a single event but a methodical, multi-faceted endeavor that touches every aspect of your operations. Let's explore the primary strategies involved in this critical shift, all of which are central to the SxSE Model.

DISMANTLING THE BOTTLENECK: YOUR JOURNEY TO OWNER INDEPENDENCE

Becoming an owner who is no longer the primary bottleneck is perhaps the most liberating and value-enhancing journey you can undertake. It's about architecting a business that can thrive and grow without your constant, hands-on intervention. This doesn't mean you become irrelevant; it means your role evolves from indispensable operator to strategic overseer and value architect. The SxSE Model provides a clear roadmap for this evolution, focusing on several key areas:

LIBERATING KNOWLEDGE: FROM YOUR HEAD TO COMPANY DNA

Over the years, you've accumulated a vast reservoir of industry expertise, nuanced customer insights, hard-won operational know-how, and intuitive problem-solving experience. This intellectual capital is immensely valuable. However, if it resides predominantly within your mind, it becomes a liability at exit. When you walk out the door, that undocumented knowledge walks out with you, potentially taking a significant chunk of the company's value with it.

Effective knowledge transfer, as envisioned by the SxSE Model, goes far beyond casual information sharing or hastily written procedure documents. It's about systematically embedding your critical knowledge into the very DNA of the organization. This involves creating robust systems for capturing, codifying, and disseminating knowledge, ensuring it becomes a durable company asset, accessible and usable by the team long after you've departed. This might involve developing comprehensive internal wikis, creating detailed process playbooks, implementing mentorship programs where experienced team members (including yourself) systematically transfer skills to others, and fostering a culture where knowledge sharing is valued and rewarded.[1]

Crucially, this process also involves cultivating "decision-making skill" throughout your organization. It's not enough for your team to have access to information; they must also develop the competence and confidence to make sound, aligned decisions without constantly seeking your approval or input. This is what truly transforms your business from being dependent on your individual brilliance to being independently valuable and resilient. Think of this as building institutional wisdom, a collective intelligence that transcends any single individual.

Developing this decision-making muscle across your team requires deliberate effort and a structured approach. It's akin to strength training for an athlete—it happens progressively, with increasing levels of challenge and responsibility. Start by

---

[1]   Visit ExitFocused.com/tools for a list of exercises to strengthen your organization.

identifying the types of decisions you currently make that could serve as valuable training grounds for your leadership team and other key personnel. These might range from handling complex customer escalations and allocating departmental budgets to making strategic pricing adjustments or selecting key vendors.

For each category of decision, work with your team to create clear frameworks or guiding principles. These frameworks shouldn't be rigid, prescriptive rules, but rather outlines of key considerations, acceptable boundaries, desired outcomes, and alignment with the company's overall V/TO. They act as guardrails, guiding thinking while still empowering individuals to exercise judgment.

A graduated authority model is highly effective here. Allow team members to begin with lower-risk decisions, providing them with support and feedback. As they demonstrate competence, sound judgment, and growing confidence, they progressively increase their scope of authority to encompass more complex and impactful matters. This approach builds decision-making skills safely and sustainably.

A vital, yet often overlooked, aspect of this is to document not just *what* was decided in significant instances, but *why* that particular decision was made. Capturing the context, the alternatives considered, and the reasoning behind the choice builds a rich repository of company wisdom. This historical context helps future leaders understand the strategic thinking and make consistently good decisions as the business evolves.

Feedback loops are indispensable in this learning process. After your team makes important decisions, conduct brief debrief sessions to review and reflect on the outcomes. The focus should be less on whether the result was perfect (though that's important too) and more on the *process* used to arrive at the decision. Examine the information that was considered, the alternatives that were evaluated, the risk assessment undertaken, and the reasoning applied. By focusing on continuous improvement of the decision-making process itself, you cultivate a powerful learning environment throughout the organization. Consider incorporating cross-functional decision-making exercises, perhaps using hypothetical but realistic business scenarios that require input and collaboration from multiple departments. These exercises help team members develop a broader, more holistic understanding of the business and learn to effectively balance competing priorities—an essential leadership skill.

Several structured methods can facilitate this systematic knowledge transfer and decision-skill development.

- Consider implementing **Decision Shadowing**, where team members observe your decision-making process in real-time as you articulate your thinking and rationale.

- Encourage the use of **Decision Journals**, where individuals document their own key decisions, the factors they considered, and the outcomes, creating a personal log for review, reflection, and learning.

- Develop and implement **Progressive Authority Frameworks** that formally define who has the authority to make what decisions at each level of the organization, with clear criteria for advancing to higher levels of authority as skills and experience grow.

- Build a library of internal **Case Studies** derived from past company situations—successes and failures—to serve as practical learning tools for current and future leaders.

- Actively foster **Mentoring Relationships**, pairing seasoned individuals with those who are developing, to facilitate the transfer of that often implicit, intuitive knowledge that is so hard to capture in documents.

- Utilize appropriate **Knowledge Management Systems**— from well-organized shared drives and intranets to dedicated knowledge management software—to store decision frameworks, process documentation, case studies, and decision rationale.

- Where appropriate, supplement these internal efforts with **External Training** programs focused on critical thinking, strategic decision-making, risk assessment, or industry-specific knowledge that can further enhance your team's capabilities.

By methodically and intentionally transferring your unique knowledge and systematically building robust decision-making skills throughout your organization, you are doing something profound: you are integrating your individual expertise into the very fabric of the company, transforming it from a personal attribute into a lasting organizational asset. This is a cornerstone of building a truly Exit-Ready enterprise.

TRANSFERRING KEY RELATIONSHIPS

Your personal connections—those carefully cultivated relationships with major customers, critical suppliers, influential industry partners, and key community leaders—are undoubtedly significant assets. They may have taken years, even decades, to build and represent a substantial amount of goodwill and business advantage. However, if the strength and continuity of these vital relationships are tied predominantly, or exclusively, to you personally, their value to a potential buyer diminishes significantly, or could even evaporate entirely, the moment you exit the business. The SxSE Model emphasizes the critical need to transform these personal connections into durable, organizational assets.

This transformation requires far more than a few cursory introductions or a quick handover meeting during a transition period. It's a deliberate, strategic, and often lengthy process of systematically embedding these relationships within the broader fabric of your company. The goal is for the relationship to be with *the company*, not just with *you*. The process typically begins with a comprehensive **Relationship Audit**. Methodically identify all key external relationships that are heavily dependent on your personal involvement. These might include long-standing customers who insist on dealing only with you, vendors who provide preferential terms primarily because of your personal history with them, or industry contacts who share valuable insights due to a long-cultivated personal rapport. For each of these key relationships, assess both its strategic value to the business and the current level of your personal dependency. This assessment will allow you to prioritize the transition efforts, focusing first on those relationships that are both highly valuable and highly dependent on you.

Abrupt handoffs are almost always a mistake. They can create anxiety for the external contact, erode trust, and potentially damage a valuable relationship. Instead, the SxSE Model advocates for a **Graduated Introduction and Transition Process**, a phased approach designed to build comfort and confidence on all sides. It might begin with you simply sharing more information internally about the key contact and the history of the relationship with the team member(s) you've designated to take it over.

The next step is to include your team member in meetings or calls, initially just to listen and learn, then gradually to participate more actively. As their familiarity and rapport grow, you can progress to having them collaborate on projects or initiatives that involve the external contact, allowing them to take an increasingly prominent lead while you gradually step back into a supporting role. This methodical approach ensures continuity, minimizes disruption, and allows the external contact to build their own trust and working relationship with your team member.

It's crucial to frame this transition positively to the external contact. Don't present it as you disengaging, but rather as the company strategically adding resources, enhancing service, or bringing fresh perspectives to the relationship—all of which benefit them. Creating **shared positive experiences** is also incredibly powerful. Encourage and facilitate opportunities for your team members to work directly with these key external contacts on meaningful projects or to solve important problems together. Collaborative success builds far stronger and more resilient professional bonds than mere social interactions or formal meetings alone.

Alongside this, maintain meticulous **Relationship Documentation**. This isn't just contact information; it's a living record of the relationship's history, the contact's preferences and communication style, significant past interactions, and any unique nuances. This institutional memory, captured in your CRM or a similar system, empowers new team members to engage effectively and appropriately, even if they weren't involved in the relationship from its inception.

Formalizing aspects of relationship management can also significantly enhance their transferability. Consider using **Relationship Mapping** techniques to visually identify key individuals within important client or partner organizations, understand their roles and influence, and map your company's corresponding points of contact. This can highlight areas of single-threaded dependency. For your most critical relationships, you might establish **Relationship Transition Teams**, formally pairing yourself (or another key executive) with a designated successor to systematically manage the handover over a defined period.

Implementing **Strategic Account Management (SAM)** programs for major clients, with clear ownership, documented account plans, and regular performance reviews, can also institutionalize these relationships. Leveraging your **Digital Relationship Management (CRM)** platform to its full potential is essential; it should be the central repository for all interaction history, ensuring that knowledge about the relationship resides with the company, not just individuals.

Finally, ensure that **contractual agreements**, where appropriate, are with the company entity, not with you personally, and that they include provisions for assignment to a successor entity, which is a standard but important detail often overlooked.

EXIT-READY ACTIONS TO BUILD YOUR EXIT-READY SUPERSTRUCTURE

The SxSE Model is a deliberate "superstructure" you layer on top of your existing EOS foundation to ensure your business is not just high-performing today, but primed for a seamless, high-value exit tomorrow.

1. **Review the Six Key Components with an Exit-Ready Lens.** With your leadership team, walk through Vision, People, Data, Issues, Process, and Traction. For each, ask: What makes this component stronger for a buyer? Where are the risks or owner dependencies? Capture insights to build a shared exit-ready perspective.

2. **Audit your EOS Baseline.** Assess where you stand today—document strengths (e.g., documented processes, strong leadership bench) and gaps (e.g., single-owner dependency, weak reporting). Summarize in a simple readiness matrix.

3. **Set initial Exit-Ready Rocks.** Choose 2–3 high-impact priorities that move you closer to readiness (e.g., "Build succession plan for key seat," "Upgrade financial reporting," or "Reduce customer concentration"). Make them Company Rocks for the next 90 days.

4. **Appoint an Exit-Ready Champion.** Assign an Integrator or trusted senior leader to act as the Champion. They own the exit-ready actions: maintaining focus, updating the matrix, tracking Rocks, and ensuring every L10/Quarterly conversation touches on readiness.

5. **Note Exit-Readiness touchpoints in your V/TO.** Without changing the V/TO structure, highlight where exit-ready considerations should be reviewed (e.g., Core Values attractive to buyers, 3-Year Picture showing transferable systems, Rocks tied to succession). Use this as a reminder to revisit those elements during quarterly and annual planning.

2

EXIT-READY MINDSET

Preparing your business for a successful and fulfilling exit encompasses far more than just operational enhancements and financial re-engineering. It demands a profound and often challenging internal shift from you, the owner. This is the "head game" of exit readiness. Frequently, navigating your own mindset, emotions, and deeply ingrained perspectives proves to be a more formidable task than addressing the tangible, business-focused aspects of preparation. Yet, mastering this internal landscape is absolutely critical for effectively steering the exit process, making sound decisions under pressure, and ultimately achieving an outcome that aligns with both your financial goals and your personal sense of fulfillment.

FROM VISIONARY-FOUNDER TO OWNER-INVESTOR

Many entrepreneurs, by their very nature, are deeply enmeshed in the day-to-day operations of the companies they've built. You're likely the chief problem-solver, the primary innovator, and the driving force behind much of what happens. However, to truly prepare your business for a successful exit, you must consciously and deliberately shift your perspective. You need to evolve from being the primary operator to thinking, acting, and making decisions like an astute owner-investor. This isn't about becoming disengaged; it's about engaging differently, at a higher, more strategic level.

This fundamental shift means methodically stepping back from the daily grind and tactical execution. It requires elevating your focus toward strategic activities that build long-term, sustainable, and, most importantly, *transferable* value. It's the classic distinction: You must increasingly work *on* the business, not just *in* it.

This evolution naturally involves delegating more operational responsibilities, genuinely empowering your leadership team to take full ownership of their domains, and concentrating your unique efforts on areas like governance, overarching strategy, and specific value-enhancement initiatives that will make your business exceptionally attractive to a future owner. You transition from being the indispensable cog to being the architect of a self-sustaining machine.

DEVELOPING A BUYER'S PERSPECTIVE

To maximize your company's value at the point of exit, it is imperative that you learn to see your business not just through your own eyes, colored by years of effort, emotional investment, and intimate knowledge, but through the cool, objective, and financially driven eyes of a potential buyer. Buyers evaluate businesses using a different calculus than owners typically do. Their primary focus is on future potential (market, scale, and opportunities), the mitigation of perceived risks, and the anticipated ease (or difficulty) of transition and integration. Cultivating a deep understanding of this buyer's perspective is not just helpful; it's a strategic necessity. It allows you to proactively prioritize improvements that directly address their likely concerns and to strategically highlight the specific factors and attributes they value most highly.

> *Buyers buy people and processes—that's really it.*
> —Ryan Holder, M&A Advisor

So, what do buyers typically look for? At the top of their list is **sustainable and predictable profitability**. They want to see a consistent track record of earnings and a clear path to future profits. Alongside this, they seek **clear growth potential**. A business that has identifiable and credible avenues for future expansion is far more attractive than one that appears to have plateaued. **Strong management depth** is another critical factor: buyers are keenly interested in businesses that are not overly reliant on the owner. A capable and empowered leadership team that can drive the business forward post-acquisition significantly reduces perceived "key person risk" and commands a premium.

A stable and diversified customer base is also highly valued, as it indicates revenue resilience and reduces the risk associated with the loss of any single major client. Finally, well-documented, efficient systems and processes signal a well-managed, scalable operation that can be understood, integrated, and further optimized with relative ease.

> **BUYERS ARE KEENLY INTERESTED IN BUSINESSES THAT ARE NOT OVERLY RELIANT ON THE OWNER.**

These are the hallmarks of what buyers consider key **value drivers**.

Conversely, buyers are acutely sensitive to and wary of risks, often referred to as **value killers** or "deal-breakers." Heavy owner dependence is almost universally at the top of this list. If the business cannot function effectively without you, its value is severely diminished. Inconsistent, opaque, or unreliable financials are another major red flag, eroding trust and making it difficult for buyers to accurately assess performance and project future earnings. Weak or incomplete leadership teams raise concerns about the business's ability to execute its strategy and manage challenges after the sale.

High customer concentration (where a large percentage of revenue comes from a very small number of clients) is viewed as a significant risk. Inadequate or undocumented systems and processes suggest operational inefficiencies and potential integration headaches. And, of course, any unresolved legal, tax, or environmental issues can quickly derail a deal or lead to substantial valuation discounts.

Top Value Killers

✗ Heavy owner dependence

✗ High customer concentration

✗ Weak/incomplete leadership teams

✗ Unresolved legal, tax, or environmental issues

A pivotal concept in the buyer's mind is **transferability**. Can the business continue to operate successfully, maintain its performance, and capitalize on its growth opportunities without you personally at the helm? Buyers are willing to pay a significant premium for businesses that demonstrate a high degree of operational independence and a smooth pathway for knowledge and relationship transfer.

They also carefully consider **strategic fit**. A "strategic buyer," an entity for whom your business offers clear synergies, complements their existing operations, or provides access to new markets or technologies, will often pay a considerably higher price than a purely "financial buyer" (like a private equity firm focused primarily on financial returns). Understanding who your likely strategic buyers are and what they value allows you to position your company and highlight its attributes accordingly. How, then, can you actively cultivate this essential buyer's perspective?

- **Conduct rigorous due diligence** on your own business. Step back and imagine you are a sophisticated investor considering acquiring your company. Scrutinize your financials with a critical eye. Objectively assess the capabilities and depth of your team. Honestly evaluate the robustness and documentation of your systems and processes. Challenge your own growth strategy and assumptions. This kind of unvarnished self-assessment will reveal weaknesses and areas for improvement that a potential buyer would quickly identify.

- **Engage with trusted advisors** early in your preparation process. Reputable investment bankers, business brokers, and specialist M&A advisors can offer invaluable, real-world insights into current market conditions, prevailing buyer expectations within your specific industry, and common pitfalls or deal-breakers they've observed. Their objective feedback can be instrumental in helping you prioritize your preparation efforts and allocate your resources effectively.

- **Study comparable transactions**. Research recent deals involving businesses similar to yours in terms of size, industry, and business model. Analyze the reported valuation multiples, the deal structures employed, and, where possible, the specific factors that reportedly drove premium prices or, conversely, led to discounts. This market intelligence provides crucial context for your own exit planning and valuation expectations.

Who Should You Call?

EOS is built for entrepreneurial, growth-oriented companies with 10–250 employees (roughly $2 M–$100 M in revenue). From an investment banking definition, this is known as the "lower middle market."

Business brokers specializing in sub-$5M "Main Street" deals are good at finding local buyers for smaller deals—think retail, convenience stores, dental offices, etc.—and bulge-bracket or large-cap investment bankers, whose minimums often exceed $100 M and have large minimum fees, rarely service this target market. These companies that still need expert guidance on exit, instead of a mainbroker or big-bank banker, engage:

- **Specialized M&A Advisors** with dedicated lower-middle-market practices.
- **Boutique Investment Banks** experienced in $10 M–$200 M transactions.
- **Transaction Consultants** or turn-key exit-readiness firms aligned with EOS principles.

These advisors combine deep deal structuring know-how with the nimbleness to preserve your culture, accelerate due diligence, and maximize value for both you and your leadership team, all while speaking your language and staying within your scale.

Adopting a buyer's mindset doesn't mean you should neglect current operational performance or sacrifice short-term profitability. In fact, many of the improvements that enhance buyer appeal—such as strengthening your leadership team, improving financial reporting, or streamlining core processes—will also directly benefit your current operations and bottom line. The key is to consistently prioritize those actions and investments that build *transferable* value, ensuring that the strengths you cultivate today are strengths a buyer will recognize and pay for tomorrow.

> *At the end of the day, you have*
> *to go to market to know the value.*
> —Ryan Holder, M&A Advisor

THE EMOTIONAL JOURNEY OF EXIT

Selling a business that you've poured your life into is rarely just a financial transaction; it is an inherently emotional and psychologically complex journey. Acknowledging this upfront and proactively preparing for the inevitable emotional rollercoaster is every bit as important as the meticulous financial and operational planning. Underestimating or ignoring the emotional dimension of an exit is a common mistake that can lead to flawed decision-making, unnecessary stress, and even post-exit regret.

Some of the common emotional challenges that owners face during the exit process include:

- **Identity Concerns:** For many entrepreneurs, their role as "the owner" or "the founder" is inextricably linked to their personal identity. Contemplating life without that title, without the daily rhythm and responsibilities of running the business, can raise profound questions about who you are, what your purpose is, and where you fit in the world. This underlying uncertainty can sometimes subconsciously create resistance to the very exit process you're ostensibly pursuing.
- **Legacy Anxiety:** You naturally harbor concerns about the future of the business you've built. You worry about

the well-being of your loyal employees, the continuity of relationships with long-standing customers, and the preservation of your reputation and the company's hard-won values and culture after you've departed. These are valid and understandable concerns that need to be addressed in your exit planning.

- **Financial Uncertainty and Fear:** Even when the anticipated proceeds from a sale are substantial, the transition from receiving active business income to relying on investment returns and managing a lump sum of capital can create a new kind of financial anxiety. This often manifests as unrealistic valuation expectations, a reluctance to make necessary pre-sale investments that could enhance value, or an irrational fear of "not having enough" post-exit.

- **The Purpose Vacuum:** The business, despite its challenges, offers a steady stream of problems to solve, goals to achieve, and a clear sense of daily purpose and structure. Facing the prospect of life without that built-in structure and daily engagement can feel daunting, particularly if you haven't given serious thought to what will fill that void and provide a new sense of meaning and engagement.

- **Shifting Relationships:** Exiting your business inevitably changes your relationships with your employees, who now report to new leadership, with customers who may interact with different people, with industry peers, where your role has changed, and even with family members as your daily routines and focus shift.

- **Decision Paralysis or Impulsiveness:** The exit process involves a series of complex, high-stakes decisions with long-term consequences. The sheer weight of these choices, coupled with the emotional pressures, can sometimes lead to an inability to make decisions (paralysis) or, conversely, to making hasty, ill-considered choices just to get the process over with.

Successfully navigating this challenging emotional terrain requires, first and foremost, a willingness to acknowledge that these emotions are normal and to be expected. It then involves proactively addressing them through honest introspection, deliberate planning for your post-exit life, and seeking appropriate support from trusted advisors, mentors, peers who have been through similar transitions, or even a personal coach specializing in owner exits.

> **YOU ARE, AND ALWAYS HAVE BEEN, MORE THAN JUST YOUR COMPANY.**

SEPARATING YOUR IDENTITY FROM THE BUSINESS

Creating a healthy and clear distinction between your personal identity and your business identity is a crucial step, not only for your own long-term well-being but also because it directly increases the business's value by reducing perceived owner dependence. You are, and always have been, more than just your company. The exit process provides a powerful catalyst to rediscover and reaffirm that truth.

This separation process can begin by consciously broadening your self-definition. Actively focus on and invest time in the other important roles and aspects of your life—your role as a spouse or partner, parent, friend, community member, mentor, or pursuer of personal interests and hobbies. Nurture these other facets of your identity. Explore new interests and passions that have the potential to form the basis of a fulfilling post-exit life. Don't wait until after the sale to start experimenting; begin dabbling now.

As part of your operational exit readiness, gradually reduce your day-to-day involvement in the business. This not only tests and strengthens your team's capabilities but also allows you to gradually become accustomed to less direct control and a different rhythm to your days.

Pay attention to how you introduce yourself. Practice describing who you are and what you do in ways that extend beyond your business title. This seemingly small change can have a significant psychological impact.

Envision your post-exit life in concrete detail. What will your typical days and weeks look like? What activities will fill your time? Who will you spend your time with? The more clearly you can visualize this next chapter, the less daunting the transition will feel.

Connect with former business owners who have successfully navigated their own exits. Learn from their experiences, both the triumphs and the challenges, particularly regarding the identity shift. Consider working with a professional coach specializing in executive or exit transitions. They can provide invaluable guidance, support, and accountability as you navigate this often-unfamiliar territory.

KEY STRATEGIES FOR SEPARATING YOUR IDENTITY

- Broaden your self-definition
- Explore new interests
- Reduce involvement in the day-to-day business
- Remove the business from your introductions
- Envision post-exit life
- Connect with other former business owners
- Work with a professional exit coach

This deliberate process of identity separation doesn't devalue your past business achievements in any way. On the contrary, it allows you to appreciate them as a significant chapter in a larger, richer life story, ensuring that your sense of self is robust and multifaceted enough to thrive long after you've handed over the keys to the business.

DEVELOPING A POST-EXIT PURPOSE

While financial security is undoubtedly a primary goal of most business exits, it is rarely, in itself, sufficient to lead to a truly fulfilling and satisfying post-exit life. Human beings are wired for purpose; we need a reason to get up in the morning, a sense of contributing to something beyond ourselves. Developing a clear sense of this post-exit purpose *before* you actually exit is, therefore, not just advisable; it's essential for a smooth and positive transition.

Begin this exploration by reflecting on your core motivations and talents. What truly energizes and drives you at a fundamental level? Is it the thrill of solving complex problems, the satisfaction of building and leading high-performing teams, the spark of creating innovation, the joy of helping others succeed, or something else entirely? Identify concrete ways to channel these intrinsic drivers and talents into new activities and pursuits in your next chapter.

Consider a variety of potential "second acts." For many entrepreneurs, a complete cessation of challenging work is unappealing. Your second act might involve consulting or advisory work, leveraging your accumulated expertise. It could be serving on corporate or non-profit boards. Perhaps it's teaching, mentoring entrepreneurs, or engaging in angel investing. For some, it might even be starting a different kind of venture, perhaps one with a greater social impact or a more flexible lifestyle. The key is to find something that genuinely excites and engages you.

Experiment and explore different possibilities before committing. Volunteer for a cause you care about. Take a course in a subject that has always intrigued you. Offer to informally mentor a young entrepreneur. These low-commitment explorations can provide valuable insights into what truly resonates with you. Talk to your family and close friends about your thoughts and ideas for your post-exit life. Their perspectives and support can be invaluable.

Don't rush the process. Finding your next purpose isn't always a linear or immediate discovery. Allow yourself time for reflection, exploration, and even a bit of unstructured "downtime" after the intensity of the sale. Sometimes, the best ideas emerge when you're not actively forcing them.

Ultimately, the goal is to craft a post-exit life that is as intentional, engaging, and fulfilling as the business you so successfully built. Getting your head right—by shifting your perspective, understanding the buyer's viewpoint, navigating the emotional journey, redefining your identity, and discovering your next purpose—is the foundational work that enables you to not only achieve a great exit but also to step confidently and joyfully into the next chapter of your life.

Here are five concrete Exit-Ready Actions to reinforce the Exit-Ready Mindset you explored in Chapter 2:

EXIT-READY ACTIONS TO CREATE AN EXIT-READY MINDSET

1. **Clarity Breaks:** Schedule a dedicated half-day each week to step out of day-to-day operations and focus on high-level strategy and value-creation initiatives. This shift from "in the business" to "on the business" is critical to evolve into an owner-investor mindset.

2. **Delegate and Elevate:** Identify three core operational tasks you currently own and hand them off to your leadership team within the next 90 days. Document clear handover plans and set regular check-ins to ensure true empowerment.

3. **Cultivate a Buyer's Lens:** Build a simple "Buyer's Checklist" of the top five factors buyers care about—sustainable profitability, growth potential, risk mitigation, leadership bench strength, and transferable processes—and score your company against it each month.

4. **Monthly Mindset Calibration:** Host a 30-minute session each month with your personal coach or a trusted Six1 Framework advisor to surface any emotional hurdles, re-align on exit goals, and reinforce the disciplined, long-range thinking that buyers expect.

5. **Keep a Buyer's Perspective Journal:** Maintain a running log of weekly observations on how a potential buyer might evaluate key areas—such as team strength, process clarity, and customer concentration—and review those insights quarterly with your M&A advisor to proactively address any gaps.

3

 **LEGACY**

EXIT VISION

Your EOS Vision Component®, powerfully captured in the V/TO, is the bedrock of your company's alignment. It ensures everyone in your organization is crystal clear on where the business is heading and the strategic path to get there. This is a monumental achievement in itself. However, the standard V/TO primarily focuses on the *business* vision— its strategy, operational goals, and execution plans. To achieve a state of true and robust Exit

> **TRUE EXIT READINESS IS AN INTRINSIC PART OF A SOUND, LONG-TERM BUSINESS STRATEGY.**

Readiness, you must consciously and strategically extend this vital component to fully incorporate an *exit* vision.

This isn't about creating an entirely separate, siloed plan that runs parallel to your business operations. Instead, it's about seamlessly integrating exit-oriented thinking into your existing strategic framework. True Exit Readiness is not an afterthought or a separate project; it's an intrinsic part of a sound, long-term business strategy.

Every significant strategic choice you make, every major initiative you undertake, has implications not only for your current performance but also for your future exit options, valuation, and the smoothness of the transition. By explicitly weaving exit considerations into the fabric of your V/TO, you create a powerful synergy, a positive feedback loop where running a great business today directly contributes to building one that is exceptionally valuable and transferable tomorrow.

Begin this integration by asking your leadership team—and yourself—a series of exit-specific questions that a standard EOS implementation might not always bring to the forefront with the same intensity.

1. What does a truly successful exit look like *for you, personally and professionally*? Challenge yourself to think beyond just a target financial number. Consider the kind of legacy you want to leave. What does the future hold for your dedicated employees? How will continuity be ensured for your valued customers? And, critically, what does your personal life look like after you've transitioned out of the business? Answering these deeply personal questions provides crucial context.

2. When do you realistically want to have viable exit *options* available to you? This isn't necessarily the date you *will* exit, but rather the point at which you want the genuine *choice* to do so, on your terms. This desired timeline will significantly influence the urgency, pacing, and prioritization of your exit preparation activities.

3. Who represents your *ideal future owner*? Consider the different categories of potential buyers: strategic acquirers in your industry or adjacent ones, financial buyers such as private equity firms, perhaps even family members or your existing management team through a buyout (MBO) or an Employee Stock Ownership Plan (ESOP). Which type of buyer would most value the specific strengths and attributes of your particular business?

Whose ownership would best align with your legacy goals and the future well-being of your team and customers? Defining this ideal buyer profile helps you tailor your preparation efforts and highlight the aspects of your business that will resonate most strongly with them.

4. How must the business operate to not just survive, but to *thrive without your daily involvement?* This question cuts to the heart of transferability. What specific operational changes, leadership development initiatives, and systemic improvements are necessary to achieve this state of owner independence?

5. Why would a discerning buyer pay a *premium* for *your* business, compared to other opportunities they might be considering? You need to clearly identify your unique, defensible, and transferable value drivers—those attributes that go beyond basic profitability and truly make your company stand out from the crowd.

Grappling with these questions and arriving at clear, honest answers brings profound clarity to what Exit Readiness truly means for your specific situation. It empowers you and your leadership team to make consistent, strategically aligned decisions that simultaneously build current operational strength and enhance future exit options and value.

ALIGNING YOUR BUSINESS AND EXIT VISION

Your overarching business vision and your specific exit vision must not be separate or conflicting agendas; they must be two strands woven tightly together into a single, coherent strategy. Misalignment between these two perspectives inevitably leads to conflicting priorities, diluted focus, and wasted effort.

When they are harmoniously aligned, however, they create a powerful, self-reinforcing momentum that propels the business forward on all fronts.

Take the time to review your current V/TO through this specific exit lens. Examine your **Core Focus**: Does it articulate a market position and value proposition that is not only compelling today but also attractive and transferable to a new owner? Or is it overly dependent on your personal skills, unique relationships, or a narrow niche that might be difficult for someone else to sustain?

Look critically at your target market as defined in your Marketing Strategy section of the V/TO: Does your current strategy build a diversified, sustainable customer base, or does it inadvertently create concentration risk that would concern a buyer? Evaluate your **Three Uniques**: Are they truly defensible and transferable competitive advantages that a new owner can leverage effectively, or are they more closely tied to your personal brand, a temporary market condition, or an operational capability that relies heavily on your specific expertise? Assess your proven process, the way you provide your services or products to your customers. Does it genuinely systematize how you deliver value to your customers in a consistent and scalable way, or does it still rely too heavily on individual heroics or undocumented tribal knowledge?

Understanding the often-subtle exit implications of each element within your V/TO allows you to proactively refine your business strategy in ways that enhance, rather than limit, your future exit options. For instance, your articulated Core Values can help you identify potential buyers who share a similar cultural ethos, which can be a significant factor in a smooth transition. Your Core Focus can point towards the types of strategic acquirers who would see the most value in your business. Your marketing strategy, particularly how it builds brand equity and customer loyalty independent of you, directly impacts the transferability of your customer relationships.

Develop specific exit goals that directly complement and support your existing business.[2] While your business goals might target revenue growth, market share expansion, or new product introductions, your parallel exit goals should focus on tangibly improving key value drivers (such as increasing recurring revenue streams or strengthening management depth), enhancing transferability (for example, by demonstrably reducing owner dependence in critical functions), and mitigating key risks (like customer concentration or supplier dependencies). These parallel goals should then be integrated into your regular strategic planning and review cycles.

Create a unified strategic narrative for your leadership team, and eventually, for the broader organization. Clearly and consistently articulate how your company's overarching strategy simultaneously drives current success *and* builds future exit value. It's crucial to frame Exit Readiness initiatives not as a sign that you're planning an imminent departure or disengaging from the business, but rather as a proactive, strategic endeavor to strengthen the business for the long term, making it more resilient, more valuable, and better positioned for any future eventuality. This narrative builds buy-in, fosters alignment, and prevents the kind of uncertainty or speculation that can arise if exit preparations are perceived as secretive or solely for the owner's benefit.

True alignment doesn't mean compromising your core business strategy or making suboptimal decisions today solely for the sake of a hypothetical future exit. It means building a fundamentally strong, resilient, and sustainable business that,

---

[2]   "Exit goals" represents EOS initiatives that may show up in the 10-Year Target/BHAG, 3-Year Picture, 1-Year Plan/Goals, or 90-Day World®, or Rocks.

by its very nature and design, becomes highly valuable and readily transferable when the time is right.

SETTING SPECIFIC EXIT GOALS AND A REALISTIC TIMELINE

Vague intentions or generalized aspirations to "be ready to exit someday" rarely translate into concrete results. Achieving a state of genuine Exit Readiness requires the same level of discipline and specificity that you apply to your operational goals and Rocks. This means setting concrete, measurable exit goals and establishing a clear, realistic timeline for their achievement.

First, work with your leadership team and key advisors to define what Exit-Ready specifically means for your business and for you personally.

- What specific valuation range are you realistically targeting, and what key financial metrics (like EBITDA multiples) will support that?
- What quantifiable level of owner independence must be achieved across key functions?
- What specific business risks (e.g., customer concentration, lack of documented processes) need to be demonstrably reduced or eliminated?
- From a personal perspective, what financial independence number must be met to support your desired post-exit lifestyle?
- What does that post-exit life actually look like in terms of activity, engagement, and purpose? Making this definition as tangible and measurable as possible is the first step towards achieving it.

Next, establish a realistic timeline for achieving this defined state of Exit Readiness. For most businesses, preparing thoroughly takes time—typically three to five years, although this can vary significantly based on the company's starting point, complexity, and the intensity of effort applied. Set a target date by which you aim to achieve full readiness, and then work backward to define intermediate **Mile-Markers** for key achievements along the way.[3] These mile-markers break the larger Exit Goals into more manageable phases (e.g., "Leadership team fully capable of independent day-to-day operations by Year 2," or "Complete documentation and systematization of all core business processes by the end of Q3, Year 1").

It's critically important to distinguish between the timeline for *achieving* Exit Readiness and the timeline for *actually executing* an exit. The primary goal of this preparation phase is to build the *option* to exit successfully, on your terms, according to your readiness timeline. Whether and when you ultimately *choose* to exercise that option will depend on a confluence of factors, including your personal readiness, prevailing market conditions, and the emergence of strategic opportunities. This clear separation often reduces the emotional pressure and perceived urgency sometimes associated with exit planning, allowing for more rational and strategic decision-making.

---

[3]   "Mile-Marker" represents key points along the Exit-Readiness journey.

PREPARE AS IF YOU'RE SELLING—EVEN WHEN KEEPING IT IN THE FAMILY

Even if your plan is to hand the reins to children or your leadership team, run the transition like a sale.

- **Build in liquidity.** Banks will underwrite any pay-out—early diligence prep turns them into allies, not adversaries.
- **Root out deal-killers.** Contracts, key-manager agreements, environmental or IT red flags—all can be fixed now rather than passed down.
- **De-risk the operation.** A cleaner balance sheet and tighter processes protect your successor from hidden liabilities.
- **Institutionalize best practices.** Give the next owner a ready-made playbook for day-one success.
- **Stay exit-ready.** Whether it's one of the "5 Ds" or an attractive unsolicited offer, your company can change hands smoothly—on your terms.

Integrate your exit goals directly into your existing EOS rhythm. Don't treat exit preparation as a separate, off-to-the-side project that gets attention only when time permits. Instead, weave it into the fabric of your established planning horizons. Your 10-Year Target on the V/TO should reflect your ultimate legacy vision, which might include the desired state of the business long after your transition.

Your 3-Year Picture must incorporate major Exit Readiness Mile-Markers, such as achieving a certain quantifiable level of owner independence or completing significant value-improvement projects identified in your readiness assessment. The 1-Year Plan should then detail the specific, substantial exit preparation initiatives that will be undertaken during the current year.

Finally, your Quarterly Rocks must include concrete, SMART (Specific, Measurable, Achievable, Relevant, Time-bound) actions that directly advance your 1-Year exit preparation initiatives. For example, a 1-Year Plan Goal might be "Implement new CRM to systematize sales process and improve data capture," and a corresponding Q1 Rock could be "Complete initial CRM data migration plan."

Review and adjust these exit-related goals and timelines regularly during your standard EOS planning sessions, just as you do for your operational goals. Remember, achieving true and comprehensive readiness often takes longer than initially anticipated; starting early, being disciplined in your execution, and maintaining flexibility in your timeline are key to reducing pressure and maximizing your chances of success.

COMMUNICATING EXIT-READINESS TO YOUR TEAM

Broaching the topic of exit preparation with your team requires careful thought, strategic framing, and ongoing communication. Many business owners, fearing they might create uncertainty, anxiety, or demotivation among their employees, choose to avoid the subject altogether. However, silence often breeds more speculation and unease than open, honest communication. When handled effectively, discussing Exit Readiness can actually improve alignment, foster trust, and even increase engagement among your key people.

They don't like risks and the unknown. That's why they are employees. Communication removes unknowns.
—Ryan Holder, M&A Advisor

The cornerstone of effective communication in this context is to consistently frame the discussion around **Exit Readiness as a journey to business strength and resilience**, not as a signal of your imminent departure or a desire to disengage. Explain to your team that the process of building a business capable of thriving under any ownership structure—whether it's yours, a new owner's, or even the next generation of internal leaders—inherently makes the company stronger, more adaptable, more secure, and ultimately, creates more opportunities for everyone involved. It's about securing the company's future and maximizing its potential, not about abandoning the present.

Decide strategically what to communicate, to whom, and when. While transparency is generally beneficial in an EOS environment, you need to tailor the level of detail and the timing of your communications. It's usually appropriate to share the *why* (the strategic rationale for strengthening the business) and the *what* (the types of readiness initiatives being undertaken, such as improving processes, developing leaders, or enhancing systems). You don't necessarily need to share highly sensitive details, like specific exit timelines, potential valuation targets, or the identities of advisors you might be consulting, especially in the early stages of preparation. The right level of transparency will depend on your company culture, the maturity and trust level of your team, and the specific context.

Consistently focus on the benefits for the team. Address the unspoken (or spoken) "What's in it for me?" question directly and proactively. Explain how initiatives aimed at reducing owner dependence inherently create more significant leadership opportunities and career growth paths for talented team members. Highlight how stronger systems, clearer processes, and better data lead to smoother operations, less frustration, and a more empowering work environment.

Emphasize that a more valuable, stable, and resilient company offers greater long-term job security and potentially even financial rewards for employees, regardless of future ownership.

Actively involve your leadership team in the process. Don't attempt to pursue Exit Readiness in isolation. Engage your leaders deeply in developing succession plans, in the effort to document and improve core processes, and in identifying and enhancing key value drivers. Their active participation not only brings valuable perspectives and expertise to the table but also builds a crucial sense of shared ownership and commitment to the journey. When your leaders are genuinely bought in and can articulate the vision and its benefits, they become powerful ambassadors for the process throughout the rest of the organization.

Be prepared to answer tough questions honestly. Your team will likely have questions, and some of them may be direct and challenging. Be ready to address their concerns with empathy, transparency (within the boundaries you've strategically set), and a consistent focus on the positive long-term outcomes for the business and its people. Acknowledge any uncertainties where they exist, rather than offering false assurances.

Reinforce the message regularly. Communicating your exit readiness vision is not a one-time event; it's an ongoing dialogue. Use your regular EOS Meeting Pulse—your State of the Company addresses, your quarterly planning sessions, and even your weekly Level 10 Meetings—as opportunities to reinforce the strategic importance of these initiatives, celebrate progress on readiness-related Rocks, and address any emerging concerns or questions. Consistent, proactive communication is key to maintaining alignment and trust throughout the journey.

By thoughtfully integrating your exit vision into your V/TO and communicating it strategically to your team, you transform Exit Readiness from a potentially daunting or disruptive prospect into a powerful, unifying force that strengthens your business from the inside out, preparing it not just for a successful transaction but for sustained success long into the future.

EXIT-READY ACTIONS FOR VISION

In Chapter 3, you learned how to weave an explicit exit mindset directly into your EOS Vision Component by extending your V/TO to include a clear, aligned "exit vision."

1. Embed Exit Goals into Your V/TO

- During your next quarterly or annual planning session, add 2–3 specific Exit Goals alongside your business targets (e.g., target valuation range, level of owner independence, timeline for viable exit options).
- Record these goals in the 10-Year Target and 3-Year Picture sections so they drive long-term strategy.

2. Host an Exit-Vision Alignment Workshop

- Bring your leadership team together to answer the core exit questions from Chapter 3 (e.g., "What does a truly successful exit look like for you?" "Who is our ideal future owner?")
- Capture their insights in a one-pager to inform all strategic choices going forward.

3. Define Your Ideal Buyer Profile

- Flesh out the characteristics of your target acquirer (strategic, financial, family-run, ESOP, etc.).
- Update the Marketing Strategy section of your V/TO to reflect a customer base and value proposition that aligns with the buyer's priorities.

4. Align Your Core Focus and Three Uniques for Transferability

- Review your Core Focus and Three Uniques through an exit lens: ensure they emphasize transferable strengths (recurring revenue, proprietary systems, strong leadership).
- Refine any elements overly tied to the owner so they resonate with a new owner.

5. Weave Exit Milestones into Planning Rhythms

- Incorporate at least one Exit-Vision milestone or Rock each quarter (e.g., "Define and socialize our exit vision" or "Validate buyer profile with external advisors").
- Ensure your 3-Year Picture includes key mile-markers (e.g., "10-Year Target updated with exit timeline" or "Employee survey on understanding of exit vision").

By taking these steps, you ensure your company's Vision not only charts a path for current growth but also builds towards a valuable and transferable future exit.

4

⚑ SUCCESSION

THE EXIT-READY TEAM

Your EOS People Component is fundamentally about getting the Right People into the Right Seats. This principle is absolutely foundational to running a great business, and if you're operating effectively on EOS, you've already made significant strides here. However, when we view this through the specific lens of Exit Readiness, the imperative sharpens: You need to elevate this component further.

The overarching goal becomes building a leadership team and an overall organizational structure that can not only operate effectively but can also drive success and growth *without your constant, daily involvement.* Achieving this level of operational autonomy not only strengthens your business by allowing you to work *on* it at a more strategic level today but also dramatically increases its transferable value in the eyes of a potential buyer. Sophisticated buyers are willing to pay a substantial premium for businesses that

> **AN EXIT-READY TEAM, CAPABLE OF INDEPENDENT AND EFFECTIVE LEADERSHIP, IS ARGUABLY ONE OF YOUR MOST VALUABLE ASSETS WHEN IT COMES TIME TO TRANSITION.**

demonstrate clear management depth and are not overly reliant on the owner.

An Exit-Ready team, capable of independent and effective leadership, is arguably one of your most valuable assets when it comes time to transition. Building this team involves methodically enhancing several key aspects of your People Component, leveraging and building upon the solid foundation your existing EOS implementation has already established.

1. **Rigorously complete and continuously refine The Accountability Chart**. This chart is more than just an organizational diagram; it's the definitive blueprint for your company's structure, clearly delineating all essential roles and their corresponding responsibilities. For optimal Exit Readiness, ensure that this chart comprehensively represents *every* critical function necessary for the business to operate successfully.

   Pay particularly close attention to those strategic or high-level roles and responsibilities that you, as the owner, might currently handle informally or intuitively—functions like long-range strategic planning, key stakeholder relationship management, or major risk oversight. Making these often unspoken or assumed roles explicit on the chart clarifies the full scope of leadership required for the business to thrive independently. Ensure the documented chart accurately reflects the *actual* day-to-day operating structure, eliminating any discrepancies between paper and reality.

   Finally, review The Accountability Chart through a critical exit lens.

   - Does this structure make logical sense without you in your current seat?

- Could a new owner or a new leadership team step in and operate effectively within this framework?

- Does it provide clear lines of authority, communication, and accountability for ongoing success and future growth?

- Completing and refining The Accountability Chart in this manner provides the essential structural foundation for systematically reducing owner dependence.

2. **Ensure deep and unwavering GWC (Get it, Want it, Capacity to do it) alignment for every seat**. Getting the Right People in the Right Seats isn't a one-time event; it requires ongoing vigilance to ensure that each person truly *gets* their role, *wants* the responsibilities that come with it, and demonstrably possesses the *capacity* to perform that job exceptionally well.

For Exit Readiness, this GWC alignment must be particularly robust, especially for those leadership roles that will absorb responsibilities you currently hold or oversee. Re-evaluate GWC for every key leadership seat, paying special attention to the "Capacity" element as it relates to potentially expanded duties or a higher level of strategic thinking.

Identify any gaps. Where a leader clearly understands their role and wants accountability, but perhaps lacks the full current capacity to meet the future demands of that seat (especially in an owner-independent scenario), you must invest in targeted development. This might involve specialized training, focused mentoring from you or an external expert, executive coaching, or a carefully planned progressive expansion of their responsibilities. In some instances, strategic hiring may be necessary to bring in crucial external skills or experience that cannot be developed internally within the required timeframe. Strong GWC alignment across the entire leadership team is the absolute bedrock for effective delegation, operational independence, and a transferable management structure.

THE HIRING IMPERATIVE IN SERVICE BUSINESSES

If you're selling a labor-hour product—HVAC, call centers, janitorial services, home health care—you don't really scale until you master finding, training, and motivating people. One of our most recent exits achieved an all-time high valuation simply because the buyers saw best-in-class processes for screening call-center hires, custom training pathways, and performance-fueling incentive systems.

In today's market, buyers *will* pay up for a business whose playbook for attracting and keeping top hourly talent is proven, repeatable, and baked into its culture.

---

3. **Methodically and intentionally delegate significant decision-making authority**. Owner dependence often manifests most clearly as a decision-making bottleneck, where too many decisions, large and small, still flow up to you. Building an Exit-Ready business requires consciously pushing decision authority down to the appropriate levels within the organization.

- **Map the key decisions** you currently make or heavily influence.
- **Implement a plan for Progressive Authority Expansion**, beginning with lower-risk decisions

and gradually increasing the scope and impact of delegated authority as individual leaders demonstrate sound judgment and accountability.

- **Provide clear decision parameters and frameworks**, defining boundaries, criteria, and desired outcomes, rather than requiring your team to seek case-by-case approval for every action.

- **Shift your role from being the pre-approver of all decisions to conducting post-decision reviews** that focus on the quality of the decision-making process, the rationale employed, and the lessons learned.

Cultivating strong decision-making capabilities throughout the organization not only improves operational efficiency and agility today but also powerfully demonstrates the business's transferability to a future owner.

4. **Implement formal and planned Leadership Development Programs**. Don't leave the growth and development of your future leaders to chance or ad-hoc opportunities.

- Assess **Capability Gaps** for each key leader, not just in relation to their current responsibilities, but also considering the future needs of the business operating without your direct oversight.

- Create **Individual Development Plans (IDPs)** for each leader, outlining specific development goals, targeted learning activities (which could include formal courses, industry conferences, cross-functional projects, or mentorships), clear timelines, and measurable metrics for progress.

- Utilize **Progressive Responsibility Expansion** as a key development tool, giving leaders opportunities to stretch their skills in a supported environment.

- Don't hesitate to leverage **External Resources** such as executive education programs, specialized workshops, or professional coaching to accelerate development in critical areas. Investing strategically in leadership development not only improves current performance and engagement but also significantly increases the human capital value of your business at exit.

5. **Establish formal Succession Planning** for all critical roles, including your own. This isn't just about mitigating the risk of an unexpected departure of a key leader; it's about demonstrating to a potential buyer that the business has a plan for continuity and a pipeline of talent. This significantly enhances stability and is highly valued.

- Identify critical positions across The Accountability Chart—those where a vacancy would cause significant disruption or loss of capability.

- For each of these critical positions, identify and actively develop at least one or two potential successors, considering both internal talent and, where necessary, external recruitment possibilities.

- Create specific, actionable Development Plans for these identified internal successors, tailored to prepare them for the target role.

- Implement robust Knowledge Transfer Processes for these critical roles, ensuring that essential knowledge, key relationships, and critical processes are documented and effectively passed on.

Formal succession planning builds organizational resilience, reduces key person risk, and demonstrates a mature, forward-thinking approach to talent management that is very attractive to buyers.

Beyond structuring and developing the team, you must actively work to reduce dependence on your personal involvement in specific operational and strategic areas. This directly increases your personal freedom now and the business's intrinsic value later.

Focus on systematically transitioning key customer relationships that are primarily managed by you. Implement a structured transition plan, gradually introducing and empowering dedicated account managers or other appropriate team members. The goal is to shift the primary relationship anchor from you personally to the organization itself—track metrics such as the percentage of revenue generated from non-owner-managed accounts to measure progress.

Apply a similar transition process to your most important vendor and partner relationships. Assign clear ownership for these relationships within your team and ensure that all relevant history, contacts, and protocols are well-documented and accessible.

Address any areas of specialized knowledge or unique skills that currently reside predominantly with you. Methodically document this critical knowledge (through process manuals, operational playbooks, internal wikis, or databases), and actively train other team members through shadowing, mentorship, cross-training, or formal development programs. The objective is to convert your individual expertise into a transferable company asset.

Continue to push decision-making authority down into the organization, supported by clear frameworks and accountability, reinforcing your evolving role as a strategist, mentor, and coach rather than the primary day-to-day operational decision-maker.

Reducing owner dependence is rarely a quick fix; it's often a multi-year, deliberate effort. However, the rewards are substantial: enhanced operational scalability, increased personal freedom for you to focus on higher-value activities, and ultimately, a significantly higher valuation and a smoother, more successful exit when the time comes.

EXIT-READY ACTIONS FOR THE TEAM

YOUR EOS PEOPLE COMPONENT, AMPLIFIED FOR EXIT READINESS.

1. **Refine The Accountability Chart**

   - In your next quarterly planning session, rigorously complete and update your Accountability Chart.

   - Explicitly document every strategic role—especially those you, as owner, currently handle informally—so that the full leadership blueprint is clear and owner-independent.

2. **Re-assess GWC for Every Leadership Seat**

   - Conduct a fresh GWC (Get it, Want it, Capacity) evaluation for each leadership role, with special focus on "Capacity" for expanded, owner-independent responsibilities.

- Identify any gaps and set targeted development or hiring plans to close them.

3. **Delegate Key Decision Authority**

- Map out the major decisions that currently bottleneck through you.
- Launch a Progressive Authority Expansion plan. Start by delegating lower-risk decisions, providing clear decision-making frameworks, and transitioning your role to post-decision reviews and coaching.

4. **Launch Formal Leadership Development Programs**

- Assess capability gaps for each key leader—including future owner-independent demands—and create Individual Development Plans with concrete goals, timelines, and success metrics.
- Leverage mentorship, cross-functional projects, and external training or executive coaching to accelerate skill-building.

5. **Establish Succession Plans for Critical Roles**

- Identify all critical positions where a vacancy would significantly disrupt operations.
- For each, select and actively develop at least one internal (or external, if needed) successor, complete with tailored development plans and structured knowledge-transfer processes.

By tackling these actions, you'll build a leadership team and organizational structure that not only excels today but also maximizes your company's transferable value—and dramatically reduces owner dependence—when it's time to exit.

5

▲ VALUE GAPS

THE EXIT-READY SCORECARD

I n the Entrepreneurial Operating System, your Data Component is anchored by the Scorecard—that vital weekly pulse check, typically comprising 5–15 key activity-based metrics, that tells you at a glance whether your business is on or off track in its operational execution. It's an indispensable tool for managing current operations effectively and driving accountability. However, a standard operational Scorecard, while crucial for day-to-day management, doesn't fully capture the nuanced array of factors that truly make a business valuable, resilient, and ready for a successful exit.

To achieve genuine Exit Readiness, you must strategically extend your Data Component to include metrics that specifically measure and track value creation, inherent risks, operational transferability, and long-term sustainability, all from the critical perspective of a potential buyer.

This isn't about discarding or replacing your existing operational Scorecard; that remains essential for weekly tactical management. Instead, it's about adding a complementary layer of measurement—a strategic dashboard, if you will— that is sharply focused on long-term value creation and the specific attributes that enhance exit preparedness. Think of it as augmenting your tactical, operational indicators with a set of strategic, forward-looking ones. Extending your Data Component in this way means asking a different, more strategic set of questions.

- What are the specific factors that genuinely drive valuation multiples in our particular industry and market segment?
- What specific risks or vulnerabilities would most concern a sophisticated buyer looking at our business?
- How demonstrably dependent is our business's performance on my personal involvement or that of a few key individuals?
- How sustainable and defensible are our primary revenue streams and our core competitive advantages?
- What specific characteristics would make our business particularly attractive to different types of potential buyers (e.g., strategic, financial, private equity)?

By systematically measuring these exit-focused dimensions, you and your leadership team gain the critical insights necessary to actively manage and proactively improve those factors that are most important for maximizing your future exit options and ultimate valuation. This expanded view of data ensures that you're not just running the business well today but also consciously and methodically building an asset that will be highly desirable, defensible, and valuable tomorrow.

THE VACATION (NO CONTACT!) STRESS TEST

Before you list your company, prove it thrives without you:

- **1-Week Getaway.** Step away for seven days—track what stumbles, then fix it.
- **2-Week Trial.** Extend the break to two weeks—identify gaps in leadership, processes, or systems.
- **4-Week Hiatus.** Take a full month off—if operations remain smooth, you're truly sale-ready.

If you can't survive these staged absences, you're not ready to sell—unless it's to a strategic buyer who'll embed leadership in your absence.

PINPOINTING AND TRACKING KEY EXIT READINESS METRICS

Creating a robust Exit-Ready measurement system involves identifying and consistently tracking metrics across five crucial categories. Integrating these metrics into your existing data review rhythm ensures a continuous and disciplined focus on building transferable value and mitigating exit-specific risks.

1. VALUE DRIVER METRICS: QUANTIFYING WHAT BUYERS PAY FOR

These metrics are designed to quantify the specific factors that directly correlate with higher valuation multiples in your particular industry and current market conditions. Improving these metrics generally has the benefit of enhancing current profitability, significantly boosting future exit value, and increasing the number of interested buyers.

The first step is to **identify the Key Value Drivers** for your specific sector. While universal metrics, such as consistent revenue growth rate, a healthy gross margin percentage, and a strong EBITDA (Earnings Before Interest, Taxes, Depreciation, and Amortization) margin, are broadly important, each industry often has unique drivers that sophisticated buyers scrutinize. Conduct thorough research on comparable company transactions in your space and consult with experienced M&A advisors to pinpoint the 3–5 metrics that are most impactful for valuation in your specific context.

Next, **set clear improvement targets** for these identified value drivers, basing your targets on relevant industry benchmarks and your desired valuation levels. Understand what "top quartile" or "best-in-class" performance looks like for these metrics.

Crucially, **assign clear ownership** for each value driver metric to the relevant member of your leadership team, making them accountable not just for tracking and reporting, but for actively driving improvement.

Finally, **visualize trends** for these metrics using dashboards, charts, or your existing Scorecard format to make progress (or lack thereof) easily visible and a regular topic of discussion during your Level 10 Meetings or quarterly planning sessions.

FIVE SURPRISE UNIVERSAL METRICS & VALUE DRIVERS

- **Employee Net Promoter Score (eNPS)** (–100 to +100): Measured via confidential survey; target ≥ 30.

- **Process Automation Rate** (%): % of end-to-end core processes automated; goal ≥ 40%.

- **Data Accuracy Rate** (%): % of critical data entries error-free; audited quarterly, target ≥ 99%.

- **Mean Time to Recovery (MTTR)** (hours): Average time to restore critical systems after an outage; monitored continuously, aim ≤ 4 hrs.

- **Succession Coverage Rate** (%): % of key leadership roles with at least one fully trained internal successor; target 100%.

---

2. RISK FACTOR METRICS: MONITORING POTENTIAL DEAL-BREAKERS AND VALUE ERODERS

These metrics quantify specific vulnerabilities or exposures that could negatively impact your company's valuation, or in some cases, even jeopardize a potential sale altogether. Consistently monitoring these metrics allows you to proactively mitigate these risks before they escalate into major problems during the transaction process.

You need to **identify Key Risk Factors** that are particularly relevant to buyers in your industry. Common examples include high customer concentration (too much revenue from too few clients), significant key person dependence (over-reliance on the owner or a small number of individuals), supply chain vulnerabilities, or gaps in regulatory compliance.

Instead of setting improvement targets for these risk metrics, you will typically **set maximum acceptable thresholds**, defining the limits of acceptable risk (e.g., "no single customer shall represent more than 15 percent of total annual revenue," or "all core operational processes must have at least two individuals fully trained and capable of execution"). Breaching a defined threshold should trigger immediate attention and corrective action, often through an IDS session.

As with value drivers, **assign ownership** for monitoring each key risk metric and for leading mitigation efforts. Consider creating **early warning systems**, such as visual alerts on dashboards or specific triggers for discussion when thresholds are approached or breached, to ensure that critical risks don't go unnoticed or unaddressed.

3. TRANSFERABILITY METRICS: GAUGING OPERATIONAL INDEPENDENCE

These metrics measure how easily and effectively the business can operate and continue to succeed without your direct, personal involvement in day-to-day operations or strategic decision-making. A high degree of demonstrated transferability significantly increases buyer confidence and, consequently, valuation.

You should **identify Key Transferability Indicators**, which are often related to reducing owner dependence. Examples include the percentage of total revenue managed and generated independent of the owner's direct involvement, the percentage of core business processes that are fully documented and consistently followed by the team, or the number of key leadership functions that have a designated and capable successor.

Set clear improvement targets for these metrics, aimed at methodically and demonstrably reducing owner dependence over a defined period. **Assign ownership** to relevant leaders for driving improvements in transferability within their respective areas of responsibility. **Track progress visually** to demonstrate the tangible shift towards greater operational independence and a more autonomous leadership team.

4. SUSTAINABILITY METRICS: ASSESSING LONG-TERM VIABILITY AND DEFENSIBILITY

These metrics assess the durability, resilience, and defensibility of your business model and its core competitive advantages. Buyers are looking for businesses that are built to last and can withstand market shifts and competitive pressures.

You must **identify Key Sustainability Indicators** that relate to the quality, predictability, and defensibility of your revenue streams and market position. Common examples include the percentage of recurring revenue (e.g., from contracts or subscriptions), customer retention or churn rates, the strength and defensibility of your intellectual property (if applicable), or metrics related to brand loyalty and market share stability.

Set targets focused on strengthening these indicators of long-term health. **Assign ownership** for tracking and improving these sustainability metrics. **Analyze trends** in these metrics over time to gain a deeper understanding of the long-term health, resilience, and strategic positioning of your business model.

5. BUYER ATTRACTIVENESS METRICS: ALIGNING WITH ACQUIRER CRITERIA (QUALITATIVE & QUANTITATIVE)

This category is somewhat different as it often involves a more qualitative assessment, though it can be supported by quantitative data. It involves evaluating how well your business aligns with the typical criteria and preferences of different potential buyer types.

First, you need to **define ideal buyer profiles** that are relevant to your business (e.g., strategic acquirers in your industry, larger competitors, private equity groups with a specific investment thesis, etc.) and gain a clear understanding of what each type of buyer typically looks for in an acquisition target (e.g., size, growth rate, market position, profitability, strategic synergies).

Then, conduct an honest **assessment of your alignment** against these defined profiles. Are you large enough to attract interest from private equity? Do you possess clear strategic synergies that would appeal to a specific industry player? Periodically review these attractiveness factors and **identify gaps or opportunities** to improve your appeal to your most desired buyer segments. **Assign responsibility** for initiatives aimed at enhancing this attractiveness, which might involve strategic partnerships, market positioning adjustments, or achieving certain scale milestones.

INTEGRATING EXIT METRICS INTO EOS

It's crucial not to create an entirely separate Exit Scorecard that becomes an isolated and easily neglected exercise. The power of EOS lies in its integrated approach. Therefore, you should integrate these new exit-focused metrics thoughtfully and carefully into your existing Data Component and established meeting rhythms.

For your weekly scorecard used in Level 10 Meetings, continue to include only the most critical, high-frequency operational metrics needed for that immediate weekly pulse check. However, ensure that any of these weekly measurables that also have direct relevance to Exit Readiness (e.g., a key sales activity metric that drives a value driver, like new recurring revenue) are understood in that dual context. Review this operational Scorecard in your Level 10 Meeting Measurables section as usual, discussing trends and using IDS for any off-track numbers, including those with exit implications.

Reserve your Quarterly and Annual Planning Sessions for a deeper, more strategic dive into the broader set of Exit Readiness metrics (covering all five categories: Value Drivers, Risks, Transferability, Sustainability, and Attractiveness). During these sessions, review trends, assess progress against targets and thresholds, and, critically, set specific Rocks for the upcoming quarter that are explicitly focused on improving key exit metrics or mitigating identified exit risks.

Ensure that every single Exit Readiness metric has a clear owner on the leadership team who is responsible for tracking it, reporting progress, and leading the initiatives to drive improvement.

By embedding these crucial exit-focused metrics into your regular EOS processes and rhythms, you ensure that the discipline of building a truly valuable, resilient, and transferable business becomes an ongoing, integrated part of your company's operational DNA, not a separate, easily deferred project. It transforms Exit Readiness from a distant aspiration into a measurable, manageable, and achievable strategic objective.

EXIT-READY ACTIONS FOR YOUR SCORECARD

To turn your Scorecard into a true barometer of Exit Readiness, take these steps:

1. **Define your Exit-Focused Metrics.** Identify 5–10 metrics across the five Exit Readiness categories (Value Drivers, Risks, Transferability, Sustainability, Buyer Attractiveness). Then narrow to 1–3 high-leverage measures to pilot on your weekly Scorecard.

2. **Integrate into your weekly Level 10 Meetings.** Add your chosen Exit-Focused metrics to the "Scorecard" section of your Level 10 Meeting agenda. Report these with the same cadence and rigor as operational metrics, and immediately IDS any off-track items.

3. **Build a Quarterly Exit Milestone Tracker.** Create a simple dashboard that tracks longer-term Mile-Markers (e.g., leadership bench strength, process documentation, customer diversification). Review it formally at each quarterly (and annual) planning session.

4. **Assign clear ownership.** Designate an "Exit Champion" (often the Integrator or a specific leadership team member) responsible for maintaining the Exit Tracker, ensuring metrics are measured, reported, and discussed consistently.

5. **Deep-dive quarterly reviews and Rock-setting.**
   During quarterly planning, dedicate time to a
   strategic review of all Exit-Focused metrics.
   Celebrate progress, diagnose gaps, and set at least
   one Exit-Ready Rock tied directly to improving a
   Scorecard metric.

By embedding these actions into your existing EOS
rhythms—weekly Level 10 Meetings, quarterly Rocks,
and annual planning—you'll keep Exit Readiness
top-of-mind and make measurable progress toward a
transferable, high-value business.

6

DUE DILIGENCE

MANAGING EXIT RISKS

In your EOS journey, the Issues Component provides the essential discipline to Identify, Discuss, and Solve (IDS) the problems, obstacles, and opportunities that are holding your business back from achieving its vision. It's a powerful, practical tool for tackling operational roadblocks and driving continuous improvement. However, a standard Issues List, populated through your weekly Level 10 Meetings, often focuses primarily on immediate operational challenges, pressing tactical concerns, or short-term opportunities. While this is vital for day-to-day effectiveness, it can sometimes inadvertently overlook longer-term, strategic risks that could significantly impact your ability to exit successfully or could substantially reduce your company's ultimate valuation.

To achieve a state of true and comprehensive Exit Readiness, you must consciously and systematically extend your Issues Component to actively identify, prioritize, and address exit-specific risks. This means proactively identifying potential deal-killers, significant value-reducers, and likely due diligence surprises on your Issues List *long before* they have a chance to become critical problems during an actual transaction process. It's about de-risking your exit well in advance.

This extension doesn't require you to replace or alter your existing IDS process; rather, it enhances and strengthens it by adding a crucial strategic layer focused on protecting and maximizing your future exit value. Encourage your leadership team to regularly ask:

- **What potential issues, if left unaddressed, would most concern a sophisticated buyer looking critically at our business?** Think broadly across all aspects: financial stability and transparency, customer or supplier dependencies, leadership team depth and completeness, potential legal or regulatory exposures, operational scalability, and market positioning.

- **What internal weaknesses or external threats could realistically derail a future sale or lead to a significantly lower offer than you anticipate?** Consider market shifts, emerging competitive pressures, operational vulnerabilities, or unaddressed technological obsolescence.

- **What potential problems, skeletons in the closet, or areas of ambiguity might surface during a rigorous buyer due diligence investigation?** By deliberately bringing these potential exit-related risks onto your Issues List alongside your more typical operational problems, you ensure they receive the same focused attention, structured discussion, and disciplined problem-solving that IDS provides. This proactive approach transforms risk management from a reactive, often crisis-driven exercise into an integral, strategic component of building a resilient, valuable, and ultimately transferable business.

- **Are there any lingering uncertainties regarding contracts, compliance, historical financials, intellectual property ownership, or HR practices?** Early identification and resolution of key exit roadblocks—such as Owner Dependence—are essential to prevent deals from stalling. Listing these issues in your Issues List and applying IDS turns potential deal-breakers into manageable, actionable challenges.

By deliberately bringing these potential exit-related risks onto your Issues List alongside your more typical operational problems, you ensure they receive the same focused attention, structured discussion, and disciplined problem-solving that IDS provides. This proactive approach transforms risk management from a reactive, often crisis-driven exercise into an integral, strategic component of building a resilient, valuable, and ultimately transferable business.

IDENTIFYING AND SYSTEMATICALLY ADDRESSING POTENTIAL EXIT ROADBLOCKS

Certain types of issues can act as major roadblocks, potentially stopping a sale in its tracks or making the entire transaction process exceedingly difficult and protracted. Identifying and resolving these high-impact issues as early as possible is therefore of paramount importance.

A primary and almost universal roadblock is significant **Owner Dependence**. If the business heavily relies on your personal involvement, unique skills, indispensable relationships, or singular decision-making authority, its transferability—and thus its value to an external buyer—is severely limited. Use the IDS process to systematically tackle specific dependencies that you've previously identified (perhaps through your work on the People and Process Components), such as those related to key customer relationships, specialized technical knowledge, or critical operational decisions. Develop clear action plans

(Rocks) to mitigate these dependencies through delegation, systematization, training, or hiring.

Another major concern for buyers involves **Leadership Team Gaps**. Significant weaknesses in your leadership team, a lack of clear and capable successors for key roles (including your own), or poor GWC alignment in critical seats will raise immediate red flags for any discerning buyer. They need confidence in the team's ability to run and grow the business effectively post-transaction. Address specific team weaknesses, succession gaps, or identified development needs for key leaders through focused IDS sessions, leading to targeted development Rocks or strategic hiring initiatives.

Furthermore, **Financial Instability** or **Opacity** is a deal-killer. Unreliable financial statements, a history of inconsistent profitability, messy or incomplete bookkeeping, or unclear and non-standard financial reporting make it virtually impossible for buyers to accurately assess your company's true performance, value, and risk profile. Clean, credible, and transparent financials are absolutely non-negotiable for a successful exit. Use IDS to tackle any issues related to your financial systems, reporting accuracy, internal controls, or the underlying drivers of profitability and cash flow.

High Customer Concentration, where a disproportionately large percentage of your revenue comes from a very small number of customers, presents a significant risk that buyers will heavily discount for. Use IDS to brainstorm and develop actionable strategies for customer diversification, or for strengthening and de-risking relationships with key accounts by broadening touchpoints within the client organization beyond just yourself.

Significant Unresolved Legal or **Compliance Issues**, such as pending lawsuits, poorly structured or unfavorable long-term contracts, intellectual property disputes, or past regulatory failures, can be absolute deal-breakers or lead to substantial indemnities and escrows. Actively identify and address these exposures with qualified legal counsel, using IDS to track progress and ensure resolution.

Finally, **Negative Market Trends** or a **Weakening Competitive Position** can deter buyers if your industry is perceived to be in decline or if your company's competitive advantages are eroding or unclear. Use IDS to explore strategic pivots, new market opportunities, or initiatives to strengthen your differentiation and value proposition.

Bringing these potential roadblocks onto your Issues List and subjecting them to the rigor of IDS forces methodical discussion, collaborative solution development, and accountable execution, systematically turning potential deal-breakers into manageable challenges or even new opportunities.

MITIGATING RISKS THAT ERODE VALUE: PROTECTING YOUR FINANCIAL OUTCOME

Beyond outright roadblocks that could halt a deal, numerous other factors can significantly reduce the potential valuation that buyers are willing to offer. Actively identifying and mitigating these "value-killers" is crucial for protecting your ultimate financial outcome from the sale. For instance, a track record of **Declining** or **Highly Inconsistent Profitability and Margins** will raise serious concerns about the sustainability of earnings and will inevitably lead to lower valuation multiples. Use IDS to diagnose the root causes of such trends and to implement corrective actions aimed at stabilizing and improving financial performance.

Weak or **Risky Contractual Foundations**, such as a preponderance of poorly written, easily cancellable, or unfavorable customer or supplier contracts, represent tangible risk to a buyer and will reduce the perceived quality and security of your revenue streams and cost structure. Utilize IDS to initiate a systematic review of key contracts and to develop strategies for renegotiation or strengthening terms where appropriate.

Outdated Technology, Inefficient Processes, or **Significant Deferred Maintenance** can signal to a buyer that substantial post-acquisition investment will be required, which they will typically deduct from their offer price. Use IDS to prioritize and address critical areas of underinvestment, focusing on improvements that enhance efficiency, scalability, and reduce future capital expenditure requirements for a new owner.

A **Poor Brand Reputation** or **Negative Market Perception**, whether deserved or not, can significantly harm buyer perception and limit interest. Use IDS to identify the causes of any reputational issues and develop and implement strategies to address them and strengthen your market positioning.

Lastly, **Hidden** or **Unquantified Liabilities** or **Contingencies**, such as underfunded pension obligations, uncertain tax exposures, or unresolved warranty claims, create significant anxiety for buyers and will almost certainly lead to valuation discounts or onerous escrow requirements. Use IDS to proactively identify, quantify, and address these potential liabilities with the help of appropriate professional advisors.

Addressing these various value-reducing factors methodically through IDS *before* you even contemplate entering a formal sale process allows you to present a much cleaner, stronger, and more valuable business to the market, thereby maximizing the price you are likely to achieve.

GREEN ICEBERGS: UNMASKING ENVIRONMENTAL LIABILITIES BELOW THE SURFACE

Hidden environmental issues often emerge during assessments, revealing costly cleanup obligations that shock buyers and trigger renegotiations. Even minor permit lapses or aging tank failures can balloon remediation estimates, eroding confidence and forcing price reductions or indemnity holdbacks. In many cases, these "green icebergs" stall diligence, shift leverage to the buyer, or collapse the deal outright. By surfacing and addressing environmental risks early, sellers keep their transactions on track.

- **Contaminated Footprint.** Historical spills, leaks, or hazardous residues that demand cleanup.

- **Permit and Compliance Lapses.** Expired or missing environmental permits that draw fines and shutdowns.

- **Emissions and Discharge Deviations.** Air, water, or waste releases outside regulatory limits, inviting enforcement.

- **Aging Hazardous Infrastructure.** Tanks, pipes, or equipment corroded or unmaintained—prime leak risks.

- **Coverage and Indemnity Gaps.** Insurance limits and contract clauses that leave environmental exposures unprotected.

Performing these checks today derisks your deal and protects the buyer (even if that buyer is your successor).

PREPARING FOR THE RIGORS OF DUE DILIGENCE: NO SURPRISES

Due diligence is the buyer's intensive and exhaustive investigation into every facet of your business—financial, legal, operational, commercial, and more. It's the phase where they meticulously verify all the claims you've made and diligently search for any undisclosed problems or risks. Surprises discovered by the buyer during due diligence are one of the primary causes of deals falling apart late in the process or prices being significantly renegotiated downwards. Therefore, preparing thoroughly and proactively for due diligence is not just advisable; it's essential.

Get your house in order *now*. Don't wait until you have a letter of intent from a buyer to start scrambling to gather information. Actively and systematically organize, update, and clean up all your key documents and records across all functional areas of the business. This includes historical financials (audited if possible), corporate governance documents (articles of incorporation, bylaws, shareholder agreements, board minutes), all material contracts (customer, supplier, employment, leases), employee records and HR policies, intellectual property documentation (patents, trademarks, licenses), insurance policies, and records of regulatory compliance. Using a comprehensive Due Diligence Checklist, often obtainable from experienced M&A advisors or found in reputable exit planning resources, can provide an invaluable guide for this process.

Think like a skeptical buyer (or their advisor). Review your own documentation and business practices with a critical and objective eye. Where are the inconsistencies, gaps, or ambiguities? What looks incomplete or poorly substantiated? What tough questions would a careful and skeptical investigation likely raise? Address these potential issues proactively, before a buyer finds them.

Consider a mock due diligence review. For many businesses, especially those anticipating a significant transaction, engaging an independent third-party firm (often an accounting or consulting firm with M&A experience) to conduct a simulated due diligence process can be an extremely valuable investment. This "practice run" can uncover potential issues and areas of weakness that you might have overlooked, allowing you to remediate them before engaging with actual buyers, and significantly de-risking the live due diligence phase.

QUALITY OF EARNINGS: YOUR PRE-SALE FINANCIAL X-RAY

Before you list your business, think of a Quality of Earnings (QoE) report as your financial X-ray—an independent, forensic analysis that goes far beyond your audited statements. Rather than accepting last year's EBITDA at face value, a QoE report normalizes one-time expenses, flags aggressive accounting. It verifies that your free cash flow supports the multiple you're chasing.

Commissioning a QoE report six to twelve months before going to market is your best defense against earnings quirks that buyers exploit—unexpected customer credits, owner perks run through payroll, or lingering lawsuit reserves give you time to correct course. With clean, adjusted numbers, you'll enter negotiations from a position of strength, reducing the risk of post-close earn-out clawbacks or price resets.

QoE delivers:

- **Normalized earnings:** Stripping out nonrecurring charges so your core profitability stands on its own.

- **Validated working capital:** Confirming the true cash tied up in inventory, receivables, and payables—no surprises at closing.

- **Audited owner benefits:** Separating personal expenses from business run-rates to avoid buyer pushback on discretionary spend.

- **Accelerated diligence:** Using a preemptive QoE report to shorten buyer reviews and signal that your financial house is in order.

- **Maximized valuation:** Since transparent, clean earnings often earn higher multiples and simpler deal structures.

A Quality of Earnings report isn't optional—it's your X-ray vision into financial risks. By investing early, you can smooth the due diligence process and command both confidence and a favorable price in the market.

Utilize a secure virtual data room (VDR) early. Virtual Data Rooms are often used for comprehensive exit planning. Begin organizing and uploading your key documents to such a platform well in advance of any sale process. This not only ensures that your information is well-organized and readily accessible when needed but also allows you to control access and track activity during the live due diligence phase. It demonstrates professionalism and preparedness.

Treating due diligence preparation as an ongoing Issue to be managed systematically through IDS—perhaps even as a recurring quarterly Rock for the leadership team—ensures that your company is always in a state of readiness. This proactive approach significantly reduces stress, accelerates the transaction timeline, protects your valuation, and instills confidence in potential buyers when you finally decide to enter the market.

EXIT-READY ACTIONS TO MANAGE RISKS

Extend your Issues Component to proactively de-risk your exit.

- **Integrate Exit-Risk questions into IDS.** In every Level 10 Meeting, dedicate time to ask: "What potential issues, if left unaddressed, would most concern a sophisticated buyer?" This ensures strategic risks surface alongside day-to-day obstacles.

- **Prioritize and categorize risks by impact.** Rate each exit-related issue—owner dependence, customer concentration, legal exposures—by its potential effect on valuation or deal flow, so you tackle the highest-impact risks first.

- **Enhance your IDS Discipline.** Don't reinvent IDS; strengthen it with an exit-lens. Treat every listed risk with the same Identify-Discuss-Solve rigor—assign follow-ups, track progress, and revisit weekly until fully mitigated.

- **Flag high-impact roadblocks early.** Add owner dependence, contractual ambiguities, IP or regulatory "skeletons in the closet," and other due diligence landmines to your Issues List long before negotiations begin.

- **Review and reset quarterly.** Use your quarterly planning session to reassess exit-risk trends, remove resolved items, and set a Rock explicitly focused on closing a top-priority risk (e.g., "Resolve contract renewal ambiguity").

By weaving these actions into your proven EOS Issues Component, you transform risk management from a reactive scramble into a disciplined, strategic safeguard of your company's value.

7

⬢ TRIBAL KNOWLEDGE

BUILD EXIT-READY OPERATIONS

I n the Entrepreneurial Operating System, the Process Component is dedicated to creating consistency, efficiency, and scalability within your business. It achieves this by compelling you to identify, document, and ensure adherence to your core processes—the fundamental way your organization delivers value to its customers and manages its internal operations. When everyone follows these documented processes, the result is a more predictable, reliable, and efficient business. However, standard process documentation, while excellent for improving *current* operational efficiency, often focuses primarily on how things are done today, not necessarily on making those operations easily and seamlessly *transferable* to a new owner or a new leadership team.

To build a truly Exit-Ready business, you must consciously extend and enhance your Process Component with a specific and unwavering focus on transferability, comprehensive knowledge capture, and demonstrable owner independence. This means going beyond simply documenting what you do to meticulously documenting it in such a way that an intelligent outsider, unfamiliar with your specific business nuances, can readily understand, replicate, and even improve upon those processes. It involves systematically unearthing and capturing critical "tribal knowledge"—that valuable operational wisdom that often resides only in the heads of experienced individuals (including, and often especially, yourself). And it means designing and refining processes that demonstrably do not rely on your personal intervention, approval, or day-to-day involvement to function effectively.

This strategic extension of your process work improves, rather than replaces, your existing EOS process disciplines. It involves asking a series of critical questions from an explicit exit perspective.

- How easily could a potential new owner understand and confidently take over our core operations based *solely* on our documented processes, without needing extensive hand-holding from current leadership?

- What crucial operational knowledge, shortcuts, or critical decision-making criteria currently exist only as unwritten "tribal knowledge" within the minds of specific team members?

- Which of our core processes still require the owner's direct input, approval, or active involvement to function effectively or to resolve exceptions?

- How would our current process documentation and adherence levels stand up to the intense scrutiny of a thorough buyer due diligence investigation?

- What specific process improvements would not only increase our current efficiency and scalability but also clearly and demonstrably enhance the business's transferable value and reduce perceived operational risk for a buyer?

Methodically addressing these questions ensures that your processes contribute not just to current operational excellence but also to building a more valuable, resilient, and ultimately sellable asset.

DOCUMENTING PROCESSES FOR CRYSTAL-CLEAR TRANSFERABILITY: THE OUTSIDER'S TEST

Effective process documentation for Exit Readiness requires you to adopt the mindset of a clear and patient teacher instructing a capable but previously uninformed student. Your overarching goal is to make your core operations readily understandable and consistently replicable by someone who lacks prior experience in your specific business or industry. To achieve this, your documentation should **assume no prior knowledge**. Write all procedures clearly, concisely, and simply, consciously avoiding internal jargon, acronyms, or assumed contextual understanding.

Where specialized terms are unavoidable, ensure they are clearly defined within the documentation itself. It is also immensely helpful to **explain the "why"** behind key steps or critical aspects of the process, not just list the sequential actions. Understanding the underlying rationale helps new owners or team members make more informed decisions and adapt the process intelligently if circumstances change.

Incorporating **visual aids,** such as flowcharts, diagrams, screenshots, or even short video demonstrations, can often communicate complex processes or decision trees much more effectively and efficiently than lengthy blocks of text alone. **Focus on your core processes**—typically the 5–10 critical processes identified during your initial EOS implementation (e.g., your people process, marketing process, sales process, core operations/service delivery processes, accounting process). Ensure these are documented with exceptional clarity, detail, and precision.

Maintain and **update all documentation rigorously** through a regular, scheduled review cycle with clearly assigned ownership for each core process. Integrate documentation updates into your standard operating rhythm, ensuring that processes are revised as they evolve.

Finally, ensure **easy accessibility** by storing all process documentation in a centralized, well-organized, and easily accessible location (e.g., a shared drive, an intranet portal, or a dedicated process management software) that is known to and utilized by the entire team. This demonstrates that your documentation is a living, breathing part of your daily operations, not an ignored relic.

Clear, complete, current, and easily accessible process documentation provides tangible proof to potential buyers that your business is well-organized, scalable, and less reliant on specific individuals. This significantly reduces their perceived operational risk and, as a result, increases the value they are willing to attribute to your company.

CONVERTING "TRIBAL KNOWLEDGE" INTO TRANSFERABLE ASSETS

"Tribal knowledge" refers to that corpus of essential skills, critical information, undocumented workarounds, and nuanced decision-making heuristics that exist only in the minds of your most experienced employees (and, very often, within your own head as the owner) and have not been formally documented or systematized. This undocumented expertise, while often a source of operational effectiveness in the short term, represents a major operational risk upon the departure of key individuals and is a significant barrier to the smooth transferability of your business. To prepare for exit, you must embark on a deliberate campaign to unearth and convert this tribal knowledge into documented, transferable company assets.

First, you must **identify where it hides**. Actively seek it out by asking targeted questions during process reviews or one-on-one discussions with long-tenured staff. Inquire about critical tasks that seem overly dependent on specific key people, procedures that appear to rely on undocumented shortcuts or "rules of thumb," or information that a new person in a role would struggle to find or understand. Pay close attention during the onboarding of new employees, as their questions and challenges often highlight these knowledge gaps.

Once identified, you must **methodically document this knowledge**. Work collaboratively with individuals who possess this expertise to translate their knowledge into clear process steps, comprehensive checklists, practical user guides, frequently asked questions (FAQs), or articles in a shared knowledge base. Ensure the knowledge holders review and validate the documentation for accuracy and completeness.

Implement **cross-training initiatives** for critical skills and knowledge areas to reduce reliance on single individuals, thereby building operational redundancy and ensuring business continuity. Where possible and appropriate, **leverage technology to embed knowledge into systems**. This might involve configuring software settings to enforce best practices, creating standardized templates or macros for common tasks, or developing automated workflows that guide users through complex processes, thereby reducing reliance on individual memory or discretion.

Converting valuable tribal knowledge from individual expertise into documented, systematized, and transferable company assets makes your business more resilient, efficient, scalable, and significantly more valuable and attractive to potential acquirers.

DESIGNING FOR AUTONOMY: BUILDING SYSTEMS THAT OPERATE WITHOUT YOU

A core tenet of business transferability, and a key attribute that buyers seek, is the demonstrable ability of the business's core operations to function effectively and consistently without the owner's constant presence, direct intervention, or day-to-day decision-making. Methodically and intentionally removing yourself from the execution of day-to-day processes is therefore a critical aspect of Exit Readiness.

Start by mapping your current involvement. Honestly and objectively assess every core process within your business to pinpoint exactly where your personal input, approval, action, or decision is currently required for the process to proceed or for exceptions to be handled. Then, for each identified point of owner involvement, determine if the task can be fully delegated to a trained and capable team member (with clear parameters and accountability), automated using appropriate technology, or if the process itself can be redesigned to eliminate the need for your involvement altogether. Empower your team by ensuring they have the necessary training, resources, access to information, and clear authority to execute these processes independently and effectively, reinforcing their ownership and accountability for the outcomes. Finally, consciously shift your role from managing execution to monitoring outcomes.

Once processes are well-documented, responsibilities are clearly delegated, and your team is empowered, trust the system you've built. Focus your attention on monitoring key performance indicators and outcomes through your Scorecard and other management reports. Use any exceptions or deviations not as reasons to jump back into the operational weeds, but as coaching opportunities to further strengthen your team's capabilities and the robustness of your processes.

Building operational systems that function effectively and efficiently without your daily intervention provides you with greater freedom, flexibility, and strategic bandwidth now, while simultaneously demonstrating to potential buyers a mature, scalable, and highly transferable business—all key ingredients for a successful and lucrative exit.

EXIT-READY ACTIONS FOR OPERATIONS

Buyers want more than revenue—they want confidence that the business will hum without you. Before you hit the market, shore up your Process Component with these Exit-Ready actions that make your operations both scalable and transferable:

- **Conduct a Core-Process Dependency audit.** Identify every point where you (the owner) must personally intervene—then for each, decide whether to delegate it to a trained team member or automate it with technology.

- **Document your top 3 Value-Driving Processes.** Create clear, step-by-step playbooks for your most critical workflows (e.g., customer onboarding, financial close, product delivery), ensuring each process is written down and accessible to the team.

- **Delegate one key process within 90 Days.** Pick the most owner-dependent task you identified, train a capable successor, and formalize ownership with clear parameters and accountability.

- **Automate or systemize a High-Volume Process.** Leverage tools (CRM workflows, finance systems, project-management software) to remove manual handoffs from at least one repeatable process.

- **Assign a "Process Champion."** Designate a team member to own process documentation, updates, and training, empowering them with resources and authority to keep your operations robust and audit-ready.

8

ADVISOR MEETING PULSE

GAIN TRACTION ON
YOUR EXIT READINESS

I n the Entrepreneurial Operating System, the Traction Component is where your carefully crafted Vision meets the unyielding reality of the ground. It's the powerful engine of execution, meticulously powered by your consistent Meeting Pulse, your quarterly Rocks, your dynamic Issues List (and the IDS process), and your insightful Scorecard. This integrated system is designed to create unwavering focus, instill profound discipline, and drive relentless accountability for achieving your most important operational goals. However, a standard Traction implementation, while exceptionally effective for *running* the business on a day-to-day and quarter-to-quarter basis, doesn't inherently or automatically focus on the specific, often longer-term, and strategically distinct execution required to become truly and comprehensively Exit-Ready.

To successfully prepare your business for a valuable and smooth future exit, you must consciously and systematically extend your Traction Component to incorporate and embed exit-specific execution discipline. This means skillfully weaving dedicated exit preparation activities, priorities, and account-abilities into your existing, well-honed rhythms of setting priorities, tracking progress, solving critical issues, and maintaining unwavering accountability across your leadership team. It's about ensuring that the important, often complex, and undeniably long-term work of building transferable value and mitigating exit-specific risks doesn't get constantly sidelined, deferred, or diluted by the urgent and ever-present demands of daily operations.

This crucial extension doesn't necessitate creating an entirely separate system or a new set of cumbersome processes; instead, it leverages the inherent power and proven effectiveness of your existing EOS tools by applying them with a clear, consistent, and strategically aligned exit-focused lens. Encourage your leadership team to consider these pivotal questions.

- How do we ensure there is consistent, dedicated focus on our multi-faceted exit preparation initiatives amidst the daily operational whirlwind and inevitable firefighting?
- What specific, measurable, and impactful exit preparation priorities should we commit to tackling as Rocks in the next 90 days?
- How will we effectively track our overall progress towards becoming comprehensively Exit-Ready over the next 1–3 years, or whatever our strategic timeframe may be?
- How do we build and maintain clear accountability for executing the diverse array of tasks and projects that constitute our exit preparation plan?

By thoughtfully and intentionally integrating exit-focused execution into your existing Traction Component, you transform the goal of building a valuable, transferable business from a vague aspiration into a consistent, measurable, and accountable part of your operations. This dramatically increases the likelihood of achieving your desired exit outcome, on your terms, and within your preferred timeframe.

SETTING AND ACHIEVING SPECIFIC, IMPACTFUL EXIT-READY ROCKS

Rocks, as you know, are the 3–7 most important, game-changing priorities for the company as a whole, and each individual member of your leadership team, to accomplish within a 90-day period. They are the mechanism that translates your longer-term vision and strategic objectives into focused, manageable quarterly sprints. To make tangible, consistent progress on your journey to Exit Readiness, it is absolutely essential that you dedicate specific, well-defined Rocks to this objective each and every quarter.

1. **Formally dedicate Quarterly Rocks to Exit Readiness**. Treat the multifaceted work of exit preparation with the same seriousness and strategic importance as any other critical business function, like sales, marketing, or operations. Aim for at least one Company Rock leadership team member Rock to be explicitly focused on advancing an aspect of your exit readiness each quarter. This ensures that dedicated resources, focused attention, and leadership accountability are consistently applied to this vital long-term objective.

2. Ensure that all **Exit-Ready Rocks are SMART**: Specific, Measurable, Attainable, Relevant, and Time-bound. Vague intentions like "Improve Processes for Exit" or "Work on Due Diligence" simply won't cut it.

3. **Assign Clear, Unambiguous Ownership**. Every Exit-Ready Rock must have a single, named owner on

the leadership team who is unequivocally accountable for its successful completion, aligning perfectly with standard EOS principles.

4. **Track Progress Diligently and Weekly**. Integrate the review of all Exit-Ready Rocks into your weekly Level 10 Meeting agenda, reporting their status (On Track / Off Track) with the same rigor and transparency as your operational Rocks. If an Exit-Ready Rock is identified as off track, immediately use the IDS process to identify the root causes of the problem and to develop and implement effective solutions.

Making Exit Readiness a standard, non-negotiable part of your Quarterly Rock-setting discipline transforms it from a nebulous, easily deferred long-term goal into a series of concrete, achievable, and accountable steps, driving consistent forward momentum.

DEFINING AND TRACKING LONG-TERM EXIT MILE-MARKERS

While Rocks provide the essential 90-day focus and execution cadence, achieving a comprehensive state of Exit Readiness is very often a multi-year journey, not a short sprint. Therefore, you also need a way to define and track longer-term milestones to monitor your overall progress, maintain perspective, and ensure your quarterly efforts are strategically aligned with your ultimate exit objectives.

Start by identifying your key long-term exit Mile-Markers. Based on your clearly articulated Exit-Ready Vision (developed in Chapter 4) and the comprehensive assessments of your business across the various EOS components from an exit perspective (as detailed in previous chapters), define the major strategic achievements required to reach your desired state of readiness. Examples might include achieving full operational independence for the leadership team, maintaining three consecutive years of clean, audited financials, successfully reducing customer concentration below a defined threshold, completing the full documentation and systematization of all core processes, or consistently achieving target scores on key value driver metrics.

Next, utilize an Exit Mile-Marker Tracker or integrate it into your V/TO. Create a simple yet effective tool—a dashboard, a strategic roadmap, or sections in your V/TO—that is reviewed at least quarterly to visualize your progress toward these larger, multi-quarter goals. This tracker might monitor progress across key dimensions, such as Leadership Team Readiness, Financial Quality and Transparency, Process Documentation and Systematization, Risk Profile Reduction, Value Driver Improvement, and Due Diligence Preparedness.

Finally, review progress on Mile-Markers quarterly. Dedicate specific time during your quarterly and annual planning sessions to formally review this Exit Mile-Marker Tracker. Celebrate the progress made, identify any areas that are lagging behind schedule, and, critically, use these insights to inform and prioritize the setting of specific Exit-Ready Rocks for the upcoming quarter.

Tracking these longer-term Mile-Markers provides essential context for your quarterly Rocks and ensures that your focused, short-term efforts are consistently and effectively moving you towards your ultimate strategic goal of being comprehensively Exit-Ready.

EXIT FOCUS IN YOUR MEETING PULSE

The relentless demands of daily operations and the constant barrage of urgent issues can easily crowd out the necessary focus on longer-term strategic initiatives, like comprehensive exit preparation. To counteract this natural tendency, you must intentionally and systematically build exit readiness discussions and accountabilities into your regular meeting rhythms to maintain consistent momentum.

First, integrate into your weekly Level 10 Meetings by leveraging your existing L10 structure. Briefly include any relevant Exit-Ready Scorecard metrics that require weekly attention, report succinctly on the status of all active Exit-Ready Rocks, and ensure that any significant exit-related problems or obstacles are added to the Issues List for timely IDS.

Depending on the current intensity and complexity of your exit preparation efforts, you might also consider a dedicated Exit Readiness check-in meeting. This could be a monthly or quarterly session, allowing for a deeper dive than is typically possible in a weekly L10. Such a meeting could be used to review the Exit Milestone Tracker in detail, discuss trends in your broader Exit-Ready Scorecard metrics, conduct strategic IDS sessions on major exit-related challenges, review input from external advisors (such as M&A specialists or wealth planners), and assign specific exit-related to-dos.

Importantly, assign clear accountability for maintaining focus. Make a specific leader on your team (often the EOS Integrator™ or a designated "Exit Champion") explicitly responsible for ensuring that exit readiness topics consistently appear on relevant meeting agendas and that progress against plans is consistently tracked and reported.

By thoughtfully embedding Exit Readiness into your established Traction tools and meeting cadences, you create the sustained, disciplined focus required to successfully manage the complex, multi-faceted journey from your current operational state to a successfully transferable, high-value business, fully prepared for its next chapter.

EXIT-READY ACTIONS TO GAIN TRACTION ON YOUR EXIT READINESS

Leverage your existing Traction rhythms to embed exit-focused execution.

- **Add an "Exit Readiness Pulse" to Level 10 Meetings.** Insert a recurring agenda item for quick updates on Exit-Focused Rocks, Scorecard KPIs, and any new exit-specific IDS issues.

- **Expand your Scorecard with Exit Metrics.** Identify 1–2 weekly measurables (e.g., percent of core processes documented, leadership bench depth) that signal your progress toward transferability—and make them part of your data review.

- **Use IDS to tackle Exit-Critical issues.** Any obstacle standing between you and a smooth exit gets its own Issues List entry—with a clear owner and deadline—so nothing slips through the cracks.

- **Embed an Exit-Focused Rock each quarter.** At every quarterly planning session, commit at least one Company Rock or Leadership Team Rock explicitly to an exit readiness milestone (e.g., "Delegate owner-only decision X" or "Document Core Process Y").

- **Designate an Exit Champion.** Assign a leadership team member (often your Integrator) to own the exit agenda—scheduling reviews, tracking metrics, and ensuring traction continues until you're fully exit-ready.

By weaving these actions into your proven Traction tools—Level 10 Meetings, Rocks, Scorecard, and IDS—you create the disciplined, sustained focus necessary to drive your business decisively toward a high-value, transferable exit.

PART 2

Six1

9

THE OPERATING SYSTEM (EOS)

I f you're reading this book, chances are you're already deeply familiar with the Entrepreneurial Operating System. You've likely experienced firsthand its transformative power in bringing Vision, Traction, and Healthy team dynamics to your organization. EOS is a comprehensive, proven system that has helped thousands of entrepreneurs get what they want from their businesses. It provides a complete set of simple, practical tools to help you clarify, simplify, and achieve your vision. This very foundation, the discipline and clarity you've cultivated through EOS, is not just beneficial for running a great business day-to-day; it is the absolute bedrock upon which true and sustainable Exit Readiness is built.

Many entrepreneurs mistakenly believe that preparing for an exit is a separate, distinct activity, something to be bolted on or worried about only when a sale is imminent. This couldn't be further from the truth. The reality is that the core principles and disciplines embedded within EOS are inherently aligned with creating a business that is attractive, valuable, and transferable to a potential buyer.

Think about it: a company with a clear, shared vision that everyone is executing on.

- The Right People in the Right Seats, all GWC-ing their roles
- A robust Data Component providing transparent insights into performance
- A proactive Issues Component for identifying and solving problems effectively
- Well-documented and consistently followed core processes
- The unwavering Traction that comes from disciplined execution

These are precisely the attributes that sophisticated buyers actively seek and are willing to pay a premium for.

Your EOS implementation isn't something you set aside when you start thinking about your exit; rather, it's the engine you supercharge. The SxSE system is designed to seamlessly extend and enhance it, layering in the specific considerations, tools, and advisory relationships necessary to navigate the complexities of an exit while leveraging the strengths you've already built.

HOW EOS SERVES AS THE INDISPENSABLE FOUNDATION FOR EXIT READINESS

Let's break down how each of the Six Key Components of EOS directly contributes to making your business more Exit-Ready:

1. **Vision Component:** A clearly articulated and shared Vision, documented in your V/TO, provides strategic

direction and alignment. For a buyer, this demonstrates a well-thought-out future for the company, reducing uncertainty and showcasing growth potential. An Exit-Ready business has a V/TO that not only guides current operations but also implicitly outlines the ongoing value proposition that a new owner can inherit and build upon.

2. **People Component:** Having the Right People in the Right Seats, all understanding their roles and responsibilities as defined on The Accountability Chart, is paramount. Buyers are investing in the team as much as the business itself. A strong, cohesive, and accountable leadership team that can operate effectively without constant owner intervention significantly de-risks the acquisition and enhances its value. The GWC principle (Get it, Want it, Capacity to do it) ensures that your team is not just present, but truly capable and motivated, a critical factor for post-acquisition success.

3. **Data Component:** Your Scorecard and other measurables provide objective, transparent insights into the company's performance. This financial and operational clarity is crucial for buyers during due diligence. It allows them to quickly understand the health of the business, identify trends, and validate your claims. An Exit-Ready business has robust data practices that instill confidence and reduce perceived risk.

4. **Issues Component:** The discipline of identifying, discussing, and solving issues effectively means your company is adept at overcoming obstacles and continuously improving. This demonstrates resilience and a proactive management culture, assuring buyers that the business can navigate future challenges. An Exit-Ready company has a strong Issues List discipline that extends

to proactively addressing potential exit-related risks and due diligence concerns.

5. **Process Component:** Documenting your core processes and ensuring everyone follows them ("The [Your Company Name] Way") creates consistency, efficiency, and scalability. For a buyer, this means the business is not reliant on tribal knowledge or specific individuals; its operations are transferable and can be scaled. Well-documented processes are a hallmark of a mature, professionally managed, and therefore, more valuable business.

6. **Traction Component:** The ability to gain Traction through Rocks, your Meeting Pulse, and consistent execution demonstrates that your company can set goals and achieve them. This track record of execution gives buyers confidence in the company's ability to deliver on its future plans and projections. An Exit-Ready business uses its Traction disciplines to systematically execute on exit preparation initiatives itself.

In essence, a well-implemented EOS framework naturally builds many of the characteristics of a highly valuable and sellable company. The journey to Exit Readiness, therefore, begins with strengthening and mastering your existing EOS implementation.

INTEGRATING EXIT READINESS DELIBERATELY INTO YOUR EOS IMPLEMENTATION

While EOS provides the foundation, achieving optimal Exit Readiness requires a conscious and deliberate integration of exit-focused thinking and activities into your existing EOS rhythms and tools. This isn't about adding a burdensome new layer of complexity; it's about applying a new lens to what you're already doing.

Consider your V/TO. When clarifying your long-term Vision, also consider how that Vision aligns with potential exit scenarios and what makes it attractive to a future owner. Your marketing strategy, for instance, should not only attract customers but also build a defensible market position that a buyer will value.

When working on your People Component, think beyond current operational needs. Is your leadership team structured and developed in a way that it could function effectively *without you*? Are you actively mitigating key person dependencies? Succession planning, often a critical aspect of Exit Readiness, becomes a natural extension of ensuring you have the Right People in the Right Seats for the long term.

Your Data Component can be enhanced with metrics that are specifically relevant to business valuation and due diligence. Alongside your operational Scorecard, you might track key value drivers, risk factors, and transferability indicators that directly impact your exit attractiveness.

Your Issues List should become a repository not just for operational roadblocks but also for potential exit-related risks or due diligence concerns. Proactively IDSing issues like customer concentration, undocumented processes, or potential legal exposures long before a sale process begins can save immense headaches and preserve value.

When documenting your Core Processes, the focus should be not just on internal efficiency but also on crystal-clear transferability. Could an outsider understand and replicate your processes based on your documentation? Is critical "tribal knowledge" being captured and systematized?

And finally, your Traction Component is the engine for executing your exit preparation plan. Specific Exit-Ready

Rocks should be set each quarter to make consistent, measurable progress on initiatives like improving financial reporting, strengthening the leadership team, or preparing for due diligence.

LEVERAGING SPECIFIC EOS TOOLS FOR ENHANCED EXIT PREPARATION

Many of the specific tools within the EOS Toolbox™ are directly applicable or can be easily adapted to enhance your exit preparation efforts:

- **The Accountability Chart:** Ensures clarity on roles and responsibilities, which is vital for demonstrating a well-structured organization to buyers. It also helps identify any functions that are overly dependent on the owner.

- **The People Analyzer:** Helps ensure you have the Right People, who live your Core Values and are strong in their roles—a key factor in team quality, which buyers scrutinize.

- **The Scorecard:** Can be augmented with exit-specific measurables that track progress on value enhancement and risk reduction.

- **The Issues List & IDS:** Perfect for proactively identifying and resolving potential deal-breakers or due diligence red flags.

- **The 3-Step Process Documenter:** Ensures your critical processes are documented for consistency and transferability, reducing reliance on individuals.

- **Rocks:** Provide the 90-day focus needed to execute specific exit preparation initiatives, breaking down a potentially overwhelming long-term goal into manageable chunks.
- **The Level 10 Meeting:** The ideal forum for maintaining weekly focus and accountability on Exit-Ready Rocks and for IDSing any obstacles that arise.

THE EOS – EXIT READINESS SYNERGY: A CONTINUOUS CYCLE

Integrating Exit Readiness into your EOS implementation creates a powerful synergy. The disciplines of EOS make your business stronger, more efficient, and more profitable today. These very same improvements inherently increase its value and attractiveness to potential buyers. As you focus on specific Exit Readiness initiatives, you'll often find they also lead to better operational performance and clarity in the present.

For example, documenting processes for transferability also improves training and consistency for current employees. Strengthening your leadership team to reduce owner dependence also empowers them to drive better results now. Improving your financial reporting for due diligence also gives you better insights for strategic decision-making today.

This isn't a one-time project but a continuous cycle of improvement. The stronger your EOS implementation, the more Exit-Ready your business becomes. And the more you focus on Exit Readiness, the more robust and effective your EOS implementation will be.

COMMON CHALLENGES AND SOLUTIONS IN THE INTEGRATION

While the synergy is powerful, some common challenges can arise when integrating Exit Readiness into an EOS-run company:

- **Short-Term vs. Long-Term Focus:** The urgency of daily operations can sometimes overshadow longer-term exit preparation.

  Solution: Make Exit Readiness a recurring agenda item in quarterly and annual planning. Dedicate specific Rocks to it every quarter.

- **Owner Bottleneck:** Even in EOS companies, the owner can remain a bottleneck for exit-specific decisions or knowledge.

  Solution: Consciously use The Accountability Chart and delegation to transfer responsibilities and empower the leadership team in exit-related areas.

- **Lack of Awareness:** The leadership team may not fully understand how their current EOS roles and responsibilities connect to Exit Readiness.

  Solution: Educate the team on the principles of Exit Readiness and how each EOS component contributes. Show them how their work directly impacts the company's future value and transferability.

- **Advisor Coordination:** Integrating external exit advisors (legal, M&A, wealth, etc.) with your internal EOS process can be challenging.

  Solution: The Six1 Framework (detailed in a later chapter) provides a structure for this. Clearly define roles and communication channels between your internal team and external advisors.

EXIT-READY ACTIONS FOR YOUR OPERATING SYSTEM

To begin strengthening your EOS foundation for Exit Readiness, consider these actions:

1. **Revisit your V/TO with an Exit Lens.** During your next quarterly or annual planning session, review your V/TO. Ask: How does our current Vision support or enhance future exit options? What aspects would be most attractive to a potential buyer? Are there elements that might need refinement to maximize appeal?

2. **Assess owner dependence via The Accountability Chart.** Honestly evaluate how many seats or key functions still heavily rely on the owner. Identify at least one function to begin systematically delegating or developing alternative leadership for in the next 90 days.

3. **Enhance your Scorecard (strategically).** Brainstorm 1–3 key metrics that directly reflect Exit Readiness (e.g., percentage of recurring revenue, customer concentration ratio, leadership team bench strength). Discuss how these could be tracked and integrated into your Data Component reviews.

4. **Dedicate an Exit-Ready Rock.** In your next quarterly planning, ensure that at least one company Rock or a key leadership team Rock is specifically focused on an aspect of Exit Readiness (e.g., "Document Core Process X for Transferability," "Develop Succession Plan for Y Role").

5. **Educate your Leadership Team.** Share the concepts from this chapter with your leadership team. Discuss how their work within the EOS framework directly contributes to building a more valuable and transferable business.

By taking these initial steps, you begin to weave the discipline of Exit Readiness into the very fabric of your EOS-run company, setting the stage for a more secure, valuable, and ultimately successful future, whatever your exit path may be.

10

YOUR LEGAL ADVISOR

As an entrepreneur steering your company with the discipline of EOS, you understand the value of structure, clarity, and proactive problem-solving. When it comes to preparing for an exit, these principles become even more critical, particularly in the legal domain. Your legal advisor is not just someone you call when trouble brews; in the context of Exit Readiness, they are a key strategic partner, one of the essential "Six Trusted Advisors" in the Six1 Framework. Their role is to help you proactively structure your business, mitigate legal risks, and ensure that your company is legally sound and attractive to potential buyers, ultimately protecting and maximizing its value at the point of sale.

Many business owners engage legal counsel reactively—to draft a contract, handle a dispute, or assist with a transaction once it's already in motion. However, an Exit-Ready approach demands a proactive, ongoing relationship with a legal advisor who understands your business, your EOS operating model, and your long-term exit objectives. They become an integral part of your strategic team, helping you build a legally robust enterprise that can withstand the intense scrutiny of due diligence and command a premium valuation.

THE PROACTIVE ROLE OF THE LEGAL ADVISOR IN BUILDING AN EXIT-READY BUSINESS

An experienced, exit-focused legal advisor contributes to your Exit Readiness in several crucial ways, long before you ever think about listing your company for sale.

1. **Optimizing Legal Structure:** They will assess your current business entity structure (e.g., LLC, S-Corp, C-Corp) in light of your exit goals, advising on any changes that could enhance tax efficiency, limit liability, or improve transferability. A structure that's optimal for day-to-day operations might not be the best for a sale, and making changes late in the game can be complex and costly.

2. **Strengthening Contractual Foundations:** Your contracts with customers, suppliers, employees, and other stakeholders are valuable assets—or potential liabilities. A legal advisor will review your key agreements, identifying weaknesses, ambiguities, or unfavorable terms that may be present. They'll help you standardize your contracts, implement stronger provisions (e.g., regarding assignability, limitations of liability, intellectual property ownership), and ensure they are consistently executed and managed. This reduces risk and enhances the perceived stability of your revenue streams and operations.

3. **Protecting Intellectual Property (IP):** Your brand, patents, trademarks, copyrights, trade secrets, and proprietary processes can be significant value drivers. Your legal advisor will help you identify, properly secure, and defend your IP assets, ensuring clear ownership and minimizing infringement risks. Robust IP protection

can be a major differentiator and value enhancer for buyers, especially in technology, creative, or brand-driven industries.

4. **Ensuring Regulatory Compliance:** Non-compliance with industry-specific regulations, employment laws, environmental standards, or data privacy rules can create significant liabilities and derail a sale. Your legal advisor will help you conduct compliance audits, implement necessary policies and procedures, and address any identified gaps, ensuring your business operates within legal boundaries and minimizing the risk of costly fines or legal actions that could spook buyers.

5. **Facilitating Corporate Governance and Housekeeping:** Maintaining clean and complete corporate records, including articles of incorporation, bylaws, shareholder agreements, meeting minutes, and stock ledgers, is essential for due diligence. Your legal advisor will help ensure your corporate governance is sound and your records are meticulously maintained, demonstrating professionalism and reducing buyer uncertainty.

6. **Advising on Employment Matters:** Issues related to employee contracts, compensation structures, non-compete agreements, and HR policies can become major sticking points in a sale. A legal advisor helps ensure your employment practices are compliant and structured to facilitate a smooth transition of your workforce.

7. **Preparing for Due Diligence:** By proactively addressing these areas, your legal advisor helps you prepare for the intense scrutiny of a buyer's legal due diligence. A "clean bill of legal health" significantly speeds up the transaction process and builds buyer confidence.

KEY LEGAL STRUCTURES AND CONSIDERATIONS THAT ENHANCE EXIT READINESS

Several specific legal areas warrant careful attention as you build an Exit-Ready business.

- **Choice of Entity:** As mentioned, is your current legal entity the most advantageous for a future sale? Discuss with your legal and tax advisors the implications of your structure on potential transaction types (e.g., asset sale vs. stock sale) and tax consequences.

- **Shareholder Agreements/Operating Agreements:** If you have partners or multiple shareholders, a well-drafted agreement is crucial. It should clearly address issues like decision-making, dispute resolution, buy-sell provisions (triggered by events like death, disability, or an owner wanting to exit), and valuation methodologies. This provides clarity and a pre-agreed framework, preventing internal conflicts from derailing an external sale.

- **Key Employee Retention and Incentive Plans:** Buyers want assurance that key talent will remain post-acquisition. Your legal advisor can help structure employment agreements, retention bonuses, or equity incentive plans (such as phantom stock or stock appreciation rights) that are attractive to employees and align with a successful transition, while also ensuring they are legally sound and tax-efficient.

- **Customer and Supplier Contracts:** Focus on terms that enhance stability and transferability. Are contracts assignable to a new owner? What are the termination clauses? Are there change-of-control provisions? Strengthening these can significantly improve the perceived quality of your earnings.

- **Real Estate Leases and Agreements:** If your business relies on leased property, ensure the lease terms are favorable and, importantly, assignable or can be renegotiated in the event of a sale.

SELECTING AND WORKING EFFECTIVELY WITH YOUR LEGAL ADVISOR: AN EOS APPROACH

Choosing the right legal advisor and integrating them effectively into your Exit Readiness efforts is key. Apply your EOS principles:

1. **Right Advisor, Right Seat:** Don't just use any lawyer. Seek out a firm or an individual with specific, demonstrable experience in M&A, corporate law, and ideally, experience working with businesses in your industry and of your size. They need to "Get" your business and "Want" to be a proactive partner in your Exit Readiness journey, having the "Capacity" to provide strategic counsel, not just reactive document drafting.

2. **Clarity of Vision (V/TO):** Share your company's V/TO with your legal advisor. Help them understand your Core Focus, 10-Year Target, Marketing Strategy, and 3-Year Picture. This context allows them to provide advice that is aligned with your overall business strategy and exit aspirations.

3. **Data Driven:** Provide them with the necessary information and access to understand your current legal posture. Be transparent about potential issues. They can't help you fix what they don't know about.

4. **Issues List & IDS:** Bring legal preparedness topics to your Issues List. If your legal advisor identifies a potential

risk or an area for improvement, treat it as an Issue to be IDSed with your leadership team and the advisor. Set Rocks to address these legal priorities.

5. **Process Component:** Establish clear processes for engaging with your legal advisor. When should they be consulted? What's the review process for contracts? Who is the primary point of contact? Documenting this "Legal Engagement Process" ensures efficiency and consistency.

6. **Traction:** Hold your legal advisor accountable for agreed-upon deliverables and timelines, just as you would an internal team member for their Rocks. Regular check-ins, perhaps quarterly as part of your Six1 Framework review, can ensure ongoing alignment and progress.

INTEGRATING LEGAL READINESS WITH OTHER EOS COMPONENTS

Legal Exit Readiness doesn't exist in a vacuum. It integrates with and supports all other aspects of your EOS implementation and overall exit strategy.

- **Vision and People:** A clear legal structure and well-defined shareholder agreements support the long-term vision and provide stability for your people.

- **Data:** Clean legal and contractual records contribute to the accuracy and reliability of the data used for valuation and due diligence.

- **Issues:** Proactive legal review helps identify potential issues before they escalate and impact value.

- **Process:** Legally sound contract templates and compliance procedures become part of your documented "Way."
- **Traction:** Legal Rocks (e.g., "Complete IP Audit by Q2," "Standardize Customer Contracts by Q3") drive tangible progress.

Furthermore, your legal advisor will work closely with your other trusted advisors—particularly your financial, tax, and M&A advisors—to ensure a coordinated approach to your exit plan. For instance, legal structuring decisions have significant tax implications, and both legal and M&A counsel will heavily negotiate the terms of a purchase agreement.

EXIT-READY ACTIONS FOR YOUR LEGAL FORTIFICATION

To begin strengthening the legal dimension of your Exit Readiness, consider these immediate actions.

1. **Schedule a proactive review.** If you don't already have one, engage a qualified corporate or M&A lawyer. If you do, schedule a specific meeting to discuss your Exit Readiness goals and ask for an initial assessment of your company's legal posture from an exit perspective.

2. **Assess your core contracts.** Identify your top 3–5 most critical customer and supplier contracts. Review them (or have your advisor review them) specifically for assignability, change-of-control provisions, and termination clauses. Add any concerns to your Issues List.

3. **Verify corporate housekeeping.** Confirm that your company's minute book, stock ledger (if applicable), and other core corporate records are up-to-date and complete. Assign a Rock to rectify any deficiencies.

4. **Review IP protection.** Make a list of your key intellectual property assets (brand names, logos, software, unique processes). Discuss with your legal advisor whether these are adequately protected (e.g., trademarks registered, patents filed, confidentiality agreements in place).

5. **Discuss shareholder/operating agreement.** If you have partners, review your existing agreement. Does it adequately address exit scenarios and buy-sell provisions? If not, make it an Issue to update it.

By proactively engaging with expert legal counsel and integrating legal preparedness into your EOS disciplines, you build a more resilient, defensible, and ultimately more valuable business—one that is truly ready for whatever the future holds, including a successful and rewarding exit.

11

YOUR FINANCIAL ADVISOR

I n the EOS world, you live by your numbers. Your Scorecard provides a clear view of your business's health, allowing you to review data regularly and make informed decisions to address issues. When preparing for an exit, this financial discipline becomes even more paramount, and your financial advisor steps in as a crucial member of your Six1 Framework team. They are not just number crunchers; they are strategic partners who help you enhance financial reporting, optimize cash flow and working capital, develop robust financial forecasts, and ultimately present your company's financial story in the most compelling and credible way to potential buyers.

An Exit-Ready business has its financial house in impeccable order. This goes beyond simply having accurate books. It means having financial statements that are easily understood by outsiders, supported by strong internal controls, and capable of withstanding the rigorous scrutiny of buyer due diligence. Your financial advisor plays a pivotal role in achieving this state of financial clarity and preparedness, which directly translates into increased business value and a smoother transaction process.

THE STRATEGIC ROLE OF THE FINANCIAL ADVISOR IN ACHIEVING EXIT READINESS

A proactive financial advisor, engaged well before an exit is on the immediate horizon, contributes significantly to your Exit Readiness by focusing on several key areas.

1. **Enhancing Financial Reporting:** While your internal financial reports are vital for running your business, they may not be in the format or at the level of detail that buyers expect. Your financial advisor will help you transition to buyer-ready financial statements, potentially including audited or reviewed financials if appropriate for your size and exit goals. This includes ensuring adherence to Generally Accepted Accounting Principles (GAAP), clear presentation of revenue recognition, detailed cost breakdowns, and transparent reporting of key financial metrics.

2. **Optimizing Cash Flow:** Consistent and predictable cash flow is a major attraction for buyers. Your financial advisor will analyze your cash conversion cycle, identify areas for improvement (e.g., optimizing receivables, managing payables, improving inventory turns), and help implement strategies to strengthen your cash position. Robust cash flow not only makes your business more valuable but also provides operational stability.

3. **Managing Working Capital Effectively:** Buyers will scrutinize your working capital needs. A financial advisor helps you understand and optimize your working capital (current assets minus current liabilities), ensuring you have enough to operate efficiently without tying up excessive cash. They will also help you establish a clear

and defensible target working capital level, which is often a point of negotiation in a sale.

4. **Developing Credible Financial Forecasts:** Buyers are purchasing your company's future earning potential. Your financial advisor will assist in developing well-supported financial projections (income statement, balance sheet, and cash flow statement) that are grounded in realistic assumptions and aligned with your V/TO. These forecasts are critical for valuation and for demonstrating the growth opportunities a buyer can expect.

5. **Improving Internal Controls:** Strong internal controls over financial reporting reduce the risk of errors and fraud, giving buyers confidence in the reliability of your financial data. Your financial advisor can help assess your current controls and recommend improvements to ensure accuracy and integrity.

6. **Identifying and Tracking Key Performance Indicators (KPIs):** Beyond standard financial metrics, your financial advisor helps identify and track KPIs that are specific to your industry and business model and are key drivers of value. This might include metrics like customer acquisition cost (CAC), lifetime value (LTV), recurring revenue rates, or gross profit per unit.

7. **Preparing for Financial Due Diligence:** By proactively addressing these areas, your financial advisor ensures that your financial information is organized, accurate, and readily available for a buyer's due diligence team. This significantly streamlines the process, reduces surprises, and builds trust.

KEY FINANCIAL ENHANCEMENTS FOR AN EXIT-READY BUSINESS

To make your business financially attractive and prepared for an exit, focus on these critical enhancements with your financial advisor:

- **Quality of Earnings (QoE) Report:** For many businesses approaching a sale, a QoE report prepared by an independent accounting firm becomes essential. This report validates your historical earnings, adjusts for any non-recurring or owner-specific expenses, and provides a clear picture of the sustainable earning power of the business. Your financial advisor can help you prepare for a QoE review.

- **Clean and Auditable Financials:** Aim for financial statements that are clear, accurate, and, if possible and appropriate for your scale, audited or reviewed by an independent CPA firm for at least one to three years prior to a sale. This adds significant credibility.

- **Detailed Financial Model:** A robust financial model that supports your historical performance and future projections is a powerful tool. It should allow potential buyers to understand your assumptions and sensitize various scenarios.

- **Normalized Financials:** Identify and clearly document any owner-related expenses or discretionary spending that would not continue under new ownership (e.g., above-market owner salaries, personal expenses run through the business). Normalizing your financials to reflect the true underlying profitability is crucial for valuation.

SELECTING AND COLLABORATING WITH YOUR FINANCIAL ADVISOR: THE EOS WAY

Choosing the right financial advisor and working with them effectively is vital. Apply your EOS disciplines:

1. **Right Advisor, Right Seat:** Your financial advisor should have experience with businesses of your size, in your industry, and ideally, with M&A transactions. They need to "Get" your EOS approach, "Want" to be a strategic partner in your Exit Readiness, and have the "Capacity" to provide insightful analysis and actionable recommendations. This might be your current fractional CFO, an external accounting firm with M&A expertise, or a specialized financial consultant.

2. **Share Your V/TO:** Ensure your financial advisor understands your company's Vision, Core Focus, and strategic goals. This context helps them tailor their advice and ensure financial strategies align with your business objectives.

3. **Data Component is Key:** Provide them with full access to your financial data and systems. Transparency is crucial for them to do their job effectively. Your internal Scorecard can be a great starting point for discussions.

4. **IDS Financial Issues:** If your financial advisor identifies weaknesses in your reporting, controls, or financial performance, add these to your Issues List. Use the IDS process with your leadership team and the advisor to develop solutions and set Rocks to implement them.

5. **Process for Financial Review:** Establish a rhythm for reviewing financial performance, forecasts, and Exit Readiness progress with your financial advisor. This

might be part of your Six1 Framework review meetings or dedicated financial review sessions.

6. **Traction on Financial Rocks:** Ensure that recommendations from your financial advisor translate into actionable Rocks with clear accountability and deadlines. Track progress in your Level 10 Meetings.

INTEGRATION WITH OTHER EOS COMPONENTS AND ADVISORS

Financial Exit Readiness is deeply intertwined with all other aspects of your business and your advisory team.

- **Vision & Data:** Your financial forecasts must align with your V/TO, and your Scorecard provides the raw data for much of the financial analysis.
- **People:** The strength of your finance team (even if it's a bookkeeper and a fractional CFO) impacts the quality of your financial information.
- **Issues & Process:** Financial discrepancies or inefficiencies are Issues to be solved, and robust financial processes (e.g., month-end close, budgeting) are critical.
- **Traction:** Executing on financial improvement initiatives requires disciplined Traction.

Your financial advisor will also work closely with your legal advisor (on structuring and compliance), tax advisor (on the tax implications of financial decisions and transaction structure), and M&A advisor (on valuation, deal structuring, and due diligence support).

EXIT-READY ACTIONS FOR YOUR FINANCIAL HEALTH

To enhance your company's financial Exit Readiness, consider the following actions.

1. **Engage an Exit-Focused financial review.** If your current financial support is primarily focused on bookkeeping or tax compliance, consider engaging a financial advisor or fractional CFO with M&A or exit planning experience to conduct a high-level review of your financial reporting and preparedness for a sale.

2. **Assess your financial reporting quality.** Honestly evaluate if your current financial statements would be clear and credible to an outside buyer. Are they timely? Accurate? Do they provide insightful analysis beyond basic P&L and Balance Sheet?

3. **Review your cash conversion cycle.** Identify one area within your cash conversion cycle (e.g., accounts receivable collection, inventory management) where you can set a Rock for improvement in the next 90 days.

4. **Begin documenting normalizing adjustments.** Start a list of any owner-related or non-recurring expenses that a buyer would add back to determine the true underlying profitability of your business. Discuss this with your financial advisor.

5. **Stress-test your financial forecasts.** If you have financial projections, review the key assumptions. Are they well-supported and realistic? How sensitive are the forecasts to changes in these assumptions?

By taking these steps and working closely with a skilled financial advisor, you transform your company's financial function from a scorekeeper to a strategic asset that significantly enhances its value, reduces transaction friction, and paves the way for a successful exit.

12

YOUR TAX ADVISOR

For any business owner, taxes are a significant consideration. When it comes to selling your business—potentially the largest financial transaction of your life—the tax implications can be monumental. A well-structured exit can save you hundreds of thousands, if not millions, in taxes, while a poorly planned one can lead to an unnecessarily large tax bill, significantly eroding your hard-earned proceeds.

This is where your tax advisor, another critical member of your Six1 Framework team, plays an indispensable role. They are not just for year-end tax preparation; in the context of Exit Readiness, they are strategic counselors who help you proactively optimize your tax position long before a sale, structure the transaction tax-efficiently, and plan for your post-exit tax landscape.

Many entrepreneurs only bring in a tax specialist when a deal is already on the table. This is often too late to implement many of the most effective tax-saving strategies, which may require years to mature or specific business structures to be in place. An Exit-Ready business, guided by the EOS principles of proactive problem-solving and long-term planning, engages a tax advisor early to integrate tax planning into the very fabric of its operations and exit strategy.

THE PROACTIVE AND STRATEGIC ROLE OF THE TAX ADVISOR IN EXIT READINESS

An exit-focused tax advisor moves beyond compliance and becomes a strategic partner in maximizing your net proceeds from a sale. Their key contributions to your Exit Readiness include:

1. **Optimizing Tax Structure:** Your business's legal entity (LLC, S-Corp, C-Corp) has profound tax implications at the time of sale. Your tax advisor, in conjunction with your legal advisor, will analyze your current structure and recommend any changes that could lead to more favorable tax treatment upon exit. For example, converting from a C-Corp to an S-Corp (if eligible and done well in advance) can help avoid double taxation on a sale.

2. **Assessing and Mitigating Tax Liabilities:** They will conduct a thorough review of your company's historical tax compliance, identifying any potential exposures or unresolved issues that could become red flags during a buyer's due diligence. Proactively addressing these minimizes surprises and potential deal derailers.

3. **Strategic Transaction Tax Planning:** Different deal structures (e.g., asset sale vs. stock sale) have vastly different tax consequences for both buyer and seller. Your tax advisor will model various scenarios, explain the

implications, and help you understand which structures are most advantageous from your perspective. They will also advise on how to negotiate tax-related terms in the purchase agreement.

4. **Leveraging Tax Incentives and Credits:** They will explore potential tax incentives, credits, or deductions your business might be eligible for that could enhance its value or reduce tax burdens leading up to a sale (e.g., R&D tax credits, state-specific incentives).

5. **Planning for Post-Exit Tax Strategy:** The proceeds from your sale will also be subject to taxes. Your tax advisor works with your wealth management advisor to develop a strategy for managing these proceeds in a tax-efficient manner, considering your personal financial goals, estate planning, and potential future investments or philanthropic activities.

6. **Advising on State and Local Tax (SALT) Issues:** If your business operates in multiple states, SALT complexities can be significant. Your tax advisor ensures compliance and identifies opportunities for SALT optimization, which can be particularly important in an asset sale where allocation of purchase price across different state jurisdictions matters.

7. **Navigating Qualified Small Business Stock (QSBS) Opportunities:** For certain C-corporations, Section 1202 of the Internal Revenue Code offers the potential for significant federal capital gains tax exclusion on the sale of QSBS held for more than five years. A knowledgeable tax advisor can help determine if your stock qualifies and guide you through the requirements.

KEY TAX CONSIDERATIONS FOR AN EXIT-READY BUSINESS

As you prepare for an exit, your tax advisor will guide you through several critical tax considerations:

- **Asset Sale vs. Stock Sale:** This is often the most significant tax-related decision in a transaction. Generally, buyers prefer asset sales for the tax benefits of a stepped-up basis in the acquired assets. Sellers often prefer stock sales, which can result in lower capital gains tax rates and avoid double taxation for C-Corps. Understanding the implications and negotiating this point is crucial.

- **Purchase Price Allocation (in an Asset Sale):** If it's an asset sale, how the purchase price is allocated among different asset classes (e.g., equipment, goodwill, non-compete agreements) has direct tax consequences for both parties. Your tax advisor will help you negotiate an allocation that is reasonable and as favorable as possible.

- **Tax Impact of Deal Terms:** Elements like earnouts, seller financing, and employment/consulting agreements for the seller post-closing all have tax implications that need to be understood and planned for.

- **Timing of the Sale:** The timing of a sale can impact which tax year income is recognized and what tax rates apply. Sometimes, accelerating or deferring a closing by even a few weeks can make a difference.

- **Pre-Sale Restructuring:** In some instances, undertaking pre-sale restructuring, such as spinning off specific assets or divisions, may be beneficial to optimize the tax outcome. This requires careful planning well in advance.

SELECTING AND COLLABORATING WITH YOUR TAX ADVISOR: AN EOS APPROACH

Choosing the right tax advisor and integrating them into your strategic planning is essential. Apply your EOS framework:

1. **Right Advisor, Right Seat:** Your tax advisor should have deep expertise in M&A transactions, business structuring, and ideally, experience with companies in your industry. They need to "Get" your long-term goals, "Want" to be a proactive planner (not just a preparer), and have the "Capacity" to provide sophisticated strategic advice. This may be a different skill set than your regular tax preparer.

2. **Share Your Vision (V/TO):** Provide your tax advisor with your V/TO so they understand your business goals and how your exit plans fit into the larger picture. This context helps them provide more relevant and strategic advice.

3. **Data Transparency:** Give them access to all relevant financial and business information. The more they understand your operations and financial history, the better they can advise you.

4. **IDS Tax Planning Issues:** Tax planning opportunities and potential risks should be treated as Issues. Discuss these with your leadership team and tax advisor, and use the IDS process to make informed decisions and set Rocks for implementation.

5. **Process for Tax Strategy Reviews:** Establish a regular rhythm for reviewing your tax strategy, especially as you get closer to a potential exit. This should be part of your Six1 Framework advisor reviews.

6. **Traction on Tax Initiatives:** Ensure that tax planning recommendations translate into actionable Rocks with clear accountability. For example, a Rock might be "Complete analysis of S-Corp conversion by the end of Q1."

INTEGRATION WITH OTHER EOS COMPONENTS AND ADVISORS

Tax planning is not an isolated activity. It is deeply integrated with:

- **Vision and Legal Structure:** Your choice of legal entity, driven by your Vision and legal advisor's counsel, is a primary determinant of your tax situation upon exit.
- **Data and Financial Reporting:** Accurate financial data, as championed by your Financial Advisor, is the foundation for all tax planning and compliance.
- **Process:** Implementing tax-efficient processes (e.g., for expense tracking, R&D documentation) can yield benefits.

Your tax advisor must work in lockstep with your legal advisor (on entity structuring, contract terms), financial advisor (on financial reporting, valuation impacts), M&A advisor (on deal structuring), and wealth management advisor (on post-sale wealth and tax planning).

EXIT-READY ACTIONS FOR YOUR TAX STRATEGY

To begin proactively managing your tax position for Exit Readiness, consider these steps.

1. **Engage an Exit-Focused tax review.** If your current tax advisor primarily handles annual compliance, consider a consultation with a tax advisor specializing in M&A and business exit planning. Ask for a high-level review of your current structure and potential exit tax implications.

2. **Model asset vs. stock sale implications.** Ask your tax advisor to provide a preliminary analysis of the potential tax differences between an asset sale and a stock sale for your specific business.

3. **Review eligibility for QSBS.** If you operate as a C-Corp (or ever have), investigate with your tax advisor whether your stock might qualify for QSBS benefits and what steps are needed to maintain that status.

4. **Identify potential tax-related deal breakers.** Discuss with your tax advisor any known tax issues or complexities in your business that could become problematic during due diligence (e.g., unresolved audits, significant state tax nexus issues).

5. **Integrate tax planning into your V/TO discussions.** During your next strategic planning session, explicitly discuss how potential exit scenarios and their tax implications might influence your long-term business strategy.

By proactively addressing tax considerations with an expert tax advisor, you can significantly enhance the net financial outcome of your exit, protect the wealth you've built, and navigate the complexities of a sale with greater confidence and peace of mind. This strategic approach to tax is a hallmark of a truly Exit-Ready EOS company.

13

YOUR M&A / TRANSACTION ADVISOR

When the time approaches to actively consider selling your business, or even just to understand its market value and potential exit pathways, the M&A/transaction advisor becomes an indispensable member of your Six1 Framework team. While your other advisors (legal, financial, tax) help build the intrinsic value and readiness of your company, the M&A advisor specializes in navigating the complex marketplace of buyers and sellers. They are your guide and chief negotiator in the intricate dance of a business sale, working to maximize your transaction value and achieve the most favorable terms.

For many EOS-run companies, the idea of engaging an M&A advisor might seem premature if a sale isn't imminent. However, even understanding the M&A landscape and what drives value in the eyes of different buyer types can provide valuable insights for your long-term strategic planning (your V/TO). A good M&A advisor can offer a market perspective that helps you shape your business to be more attractive long before you decide to sell. When you *are* ready to explore an exit, their expertise is non-negotiable for a successful outcome.

THE PIVOTAL ROLE OF THE M&A / TRANSACTION ADVISOR IN YOUR EXIT JOURNEY

An M&A advisor brings a specialized skillset and market knowledge that most business owners, even highly successful ones, do not possess. Their role in your Exit Readiness and execution includes:

1. **Evaluating Exit Options:** Not all exits are the same. An M&A advisor helps you understand the pros and cons of various exit paths, such as a sale to a strategic buyer, a private equity group, a management buyout (MBO), an Employee Stock Ownership Plan (ESOP), or a family succession. They help you align your choice of exit path with your personal and financial goals.

2. **Pre-Sale Value Enhancement Advice:** Drawing on their market experience, they can identify specific operational, financial, or strategic changes that could significantly enhance your company's attractiveness and valuation to potential buyers. This advice often complements the work of your other advisors but comes with a specific focus on what the transaction market currently rewards.

3. **Timing the Market:** While you can't perfectly time the market, an M&A advisor has insights into current M&A trends, industry multiples, and buyer appetite, helping you decide on an opportune time to explore a sale.

4. **Preparing Marketing Materials:** They will create professional, compelling marketing documents (like a Confidential Information Memorandum, or CIM) that present your business in the best possible light to potential buyers, highlighting its strengths, growth opportunities, and financial performance, all while maintaining confidentiality.

5. **Identifying and Qualifying Potential Buyers:** Leveraging their network and research capabilities, M&A advisors identify a targeted list of potential strategic and financial buyers who are most likely to be interested in your business and have the capacity to complete a transaction. They also vet these buyers to ensure they are credible and serious.

6. **Managing the Sale Process:** They orchestrate the entire sale process, from initial confidential outreach to buyers, managing communications, coordinating due diligence, soliciting indications of interest and formal offers (Letters of Intent [LOIs]), and creating a competitive environment to drive up value.

7. **Negotiating Transaction Terms:** This is a core area of their expertise. They lead or support you in negotiating not just the price, but all critical terms of the deal, including payment structure (cash, stock, earnouts, seller notes), working capital adjustments, representations and warranties, indemnification, and post-closing obligations. Their experience in numerous deals gives them an advantage in these complex negotiations.

8. **Facilitating Due Diligence:** They help manage the flow of information during the buyer's due diligence process, working with your team to respond to requests efficiently and address any concerns that arise.

9. **Closing the Transaction:** They work closely with your legal and tax advisors to navigate the final stages of the deal, from definitive purchase agreement to closing.

KEY CONSIDERATIONS WHEN ENGAGING AN M&A ADVISOR

Your M&A advisor will guide you through critical aspects of the transaction process:

- **Valuation Expectations:** While they don't set the final price (the market does), they will provide a realistic valuation range based on market comparables, your company's performance, and current M&A conditions. This helps set realistic expectations from the outset.
- **Confidentiality:** Maintaining confidentiality throughout the sale process is crucial to avoid unsettling employees, customers, or suppliers. M&A advisors have established protocols for this.
- **Deal Structure:** As discussed with your tax and legal advisors, the M&A advisor will be central to negotiating the deal structure (asset vs. stock sale) that balances buyer preferences with your financial and tax objectives.
- **Creating Competitive Tension:** A key role of the M&A advisor is to create a competitive bidding situation among multiple interested buyers, which is the most effective way to maximize your sale price and achieve favorable terms.

BEYOND PRICE

While price matters, every seller has a unique set of priorities that shape the ideal transaction. Outlining and sharing these goals early ensures that deal structures, timelines, and partner selection all align with your vision.

Key Seller Objectives Beyond Valuation

- **Transition Timeline:** Do you want a phased hand-off over months or an immediate close?
- **Cultural Continuity:** Is preserving company culture or legacy as critical as cash proceeds?
- **Employee Outcomes:** Are retention guarantees, management roles, or bonus pools top priorities?
- **Buyer Profile:** Are you targeting strategic acquirers, private investors, or family successions?
- **Post-Close Involvement:** Do you plan to stay on as advisor, investor, or board member?
- **Tax & Personal Goals:** What mix of cash, earn-out, rollover equity, or tax-efficient structuring best serves your personal plans?

By codifying and communicating these objectives—first to your advisory team, then to prospective buyers—you transform negotiations from a one-dimensional price auction into a tailored process that delivers on your full spectrum of goals.

SELECTING AND PARTNERING WITH YOUR M&A ADVISOR: THE EOS WAY

Choosing the right M&A advisor is one of the most important decisions you'll make in your exit journey. Apply your EOS principles:

1. **Right Advisor, Right Seat:** Look for an M&A firm or individual with a proven track record of successful transactions in your industry and for companies of your size. Check references thoroughly. They must "Get" your business and your exit objectives, "Want" to represent you with integrity and tenacity, and have the "Capacity" (experience, network, resources) to manage a complex sale process effectively.

2. **Align on Vision (V/TO):** Share your V/TO and your personal exit goals. Ensure they understand what a successful exit looks like for *you*, beyond just the financial number. Are you looking for a quick exit, a continued role, preservation of legacy, or specific outcomes for your employees?

3. **Data-Driven Approach:** Be prepared to provide comprehensive data about your business. The quality of their advice and marketing materials depends on the quality of information you provide. Your existing EOS Data Component will be invaluable here.

4. **IDS Process Challenges:** The sale process will inevitably have its challenges and decision points. Use the IDS framework with your M&A advisor and internal team to address these effectively. For example, how to respond to a lowball offer, or how to handle a difficult due diligence request.

5. **Clear Process and Communication:** Ensure the M&A advisor outlines a clear process for the engagement, from initial assessment through to closing. Establish regular communication protocols (e.g., weekly updates during an active sale process).

6. **Traction and Accountability:** While much of their work is market-dependent, hold them accountable for the aspects they control: quality of marketing materials, thoroughness of buyer research, proactive communication, and diligent process management.

VETTING YOUR M&A ADVISOR AND HIGH-LEVEL DEAL ROADMAP

When you first meet an M&A advisor—often before they've seen any financials—you're not looking for a guess at your company's worth. Value is set by the market, not by you or the advisor. What you need is someone who can run a rigorous lower-middle-market sale process, typically nine to twelve months long. You'll work closely with them through what may be the largest liquidity event of your life, so trust, rapport, and proven expertise are non-negotiable.

HIGH-LEVEL M&A TIMELINE (9-12 MONTHS)

- **Phase 1: Advisor selection and kick-off (0–1 month).** Interview candidates, check references, and agree on engagement terms.

- **Phase 2: Preparation and packaging (1–3 months).** Conduct due diligence, craft the confidential information memorandum, and build financial models.

- **Phase 3: Marketing and buyer outreach (3–6 months).** Distribute teasers under NDA, manage buyer Q&A, and collect indications of interest.

- **Phase 4: Buyer screening and shortlisting (6–8 months).** Host management presentations, evaluate bids, and select finalists.

- **Phase 5: Due diligence and negotiation (8–11 months).** Coordinate deep diligence, negotiate the purchase agreement, and resolve key issues.

- **Phase 6: Closing and transition (11–12 months).** Execute documents, transfer funds, and support handover to new ownership.

KEY QUESTIONS TO ASK YOUR ADVISOR

- Ask for client references and probe how the advisor handled difficult phases, what they explained up front, why any deals faltered, and whether they'd recommend the advisor to peers.

- Request professional references from M&A attorneys, CPAs, and other specialists, and ask whether the advisor prioritized client interests and collaborated effectively.

- Walk me step by step through your M&A process—ask for examples, clarify any steps that don't make sense, and ensure their playbook aligns with your objectives.

- How familiar are you with EOS and the Step-by-Step Exit framework? A top advisor welcomes input from all your trusted advisors and coordinates like a true team quarterback.

Choosing the right advisor transforms a daunting sale into a guided journey. With the right process discipline and alignment to your goals, you'll not only maximize value but also ensure a smooth transition for everyone involved.

INTEGRATION WITH OTHER EOS COMPONENTS AND YOUR ADVISORY TEAM

The M&A advisor's work is the culmination of much of your EOS journey and the efforts of your other advisors.

- **Vision, People, Data, Issues, Process, Traction:** The strength in each of these Six Key Components, which you've built through EOS, directly contributes to the attractiveness and value of your business that the M&A advisor will market.
- **Legal, Financial, Tax Advisors:** The M&A advisor works hand-in-glove with these professionals. Your legal advisor handles the purchase agreement and legal due diligence. Your financial advisor provides the financial data and supports financial due diligence. Your tax advisor structures the deal for tax efficiency. Seamless coordination is vital.

EXIT-READY ACTIONS FOR ENGAGING M&A EXPERTISE

Even if you are not planning to sell immediately, you can take steps to prepare for an eventual engagement with an M&A advisor.

1. **Educate yourself.** Start learning about the M&A process and what buyers in your industry typically look for. Attend industry conferences or webinars that discuss M&A trends.

2. **Network with potential advisors.** Casually meet with a few M&A advisors who specialize in your industry. Think of it as informational interviewing. You're not committing to anything, just building relationships and understanding their approach. Ask them what value drivers they see for businesses like yours.

3. **Get a preliminary valuation opinion (when appropriate).** If you are 1–3 years from a potential exit, consider engaging an M&A advisor or valuation expert for an informal or formal valuation. This can provide a realistic baseline and highlight areas for value enhancement.

4. **Focus on your EOS implementation.** The single best thing you can do to prepare for a successful engagement with an M&A advisor is to run an exceptionally strong EOS company. The clearer your Vision, the stronger your People, the more robust your Data, the more effectively you solve Issues, the more documented your Processes, and the greater your Traction, the better story your M&A advisor will have to tell, and the better outcome you will achieve.

5. **Discuss "marketability" with your leadership team.** As part of your strategic planning, have a conversation with your leadership team about what makes a business in your industry attractive to buyers. This can help align everyone on building long-term transferable value.

Your M&A / transaction advisor is your expert navigator through the often turbulent waters of selling your business. By selecting them carefully, integrating them with your EOS disciplines, and preparing your company diligently, you significantly increase the likelihood of achieving an exit that meets your financial goals and personal aspirations, allowing you to transition confidently to your next adventure.

14

YOUR WEALTH MANAGEMENT ADVISOR

For many entrepreneurs, their business isn't just a source of income; it's their primary financial asset, the culmination of years of effort and risk. The sale of this business often represents a once-in-a-lifetime liquidity event, transforming on-paper wealth into tangible capital. Managing this newfound wealth effectively, ensuring it supports your long-term personal and financial goals, and protecting it for the future, requires a different kind of expertise. This is the domain of your Wealth Management Advisor, a critical member of your Six1 Framework team, especially as you approach and navigate an exit.

While your other advisors focus on maximizing the value *of* your business and executing its sale, your wealth management advisor focuses on what happens *after* the sale—how the proceeds will be structured, invested, and utilized to support your life beyond the company. Their involvement should begin well before a transaction, as understanding your personal financial needs and goals can significantly influence your exit strategy, including your target valuation and desired deal terms.

THE INDISPENSABLE ROLE OF THE WEALTH MANAGEMENT ADVISOR IN YOUR EXIT JOURNEY

A skilled wealth management advisor provides comprehensive financial planning and investment management tailored to your unique circumstances, post-exit aspirations, and risk tolerance. Their key contributions include:

1. **Defining personal financial goals post-exit.** What do you want your life to look like after you sell your business? Do you plan to retire, start a new venture, travel, or focus on philanthropy? Your Wealth Management Advisor helps you quantify these goals, understand the financial resources required, and create a realistic financial plan to achieve them. This clarity is vital *before* you sell, as it helps define your "number"—the net proceeds you need to achieve your objectives.

2. **Pre-sale financial and estate planning.** They work with your tax and legal advisors to structure your personal finances and estate in a tax-efficient manner, considering the impending liquidity event. This might involve setting up trusts, gifting strategies, or other vehicles to minimize taxes and protect assets for your family.

3. **Developing a post-exit investment strategy.** Once you receive the sale proceeds, how should they be invested? Your wealth management advisor helps you develop a diversified investment portfolio aligned with your risk tolerance, income needs, and long-term growth objectives. This strategy will likely be very different from how you managed capital within your operating business.

4. **Managing liquidity and cash flow.** They help you plan for managing a large influx of cash, ensuring you have sufficient liquidity for your near-term needs while

deploying the rest strategically for long-term growth and income generation.

5. **Risk mitigation and asset protection.** Protecting your newfound wealth from market volatility, inflation, creditors, or unforeseen personal circumstances is crucial. They advise on insurance, asset allocation, and legal structures to mitigate these risks.

6. **Lifestyle planning and budgeting.** Transitioning from deriving income from an active business to relying on investment income requires a shift in mindset and financial management. They help you create a sustainable post-exit budget and spending plan.

7. **Charitable giving and philanthropy.** If philanthropy is part of your vision, your wealth management advisor can help you structure your giving in a tax-efficient and impactful way, perhaps through a donor-advised fund or a private foundation.

8. **Coordination with other advisors:** They act as a quarterback for your personal financial life, coordinating with your accountant, estate planning attorney, and insurance professionals to ensure a cohesive strategy.

KEY CONSIDERATIONS FOR POST-EXIT WEALTH MANAGEMENT

As you plan for life after the sale, your wealth management advisor will guide you through several important areas.

- **Understanding Your "Net Number":** It's not just the gross sale price that matters, but the net amount you receive after taxes, fees (M&A advisor, legal, etc.), and any debt repayment. Your wealth advisor helps you calculate this critical figure.

- **Diversification:** Moving from having most of your wealth tied up in one illiquid asset (your business) to a diversified portfolio of liquid assets is a fundamental shift and a key principle of wealth preservation.

- **Tax Implications of Investments:** Different investment types have different tax consequences. Your advisor will help you build a tax-aware investment portfolio.

- **Estate Planning:** Ensuring your wealth is transferred according to your wishes and in a tax-efficient manner is a critical component of long-term wealth management.

SELECTING AND COLLABORATING WITH YOUR WEALTH MANAGEMENT ADVISOR: THE EOS WAY

Choosing a wealth management advisor you trust implicitly is paramount. Apply your EOS principles.

1. **Right Advisor, Right Seat:** Look for a fiduciary wealth management advisor (one who is legally obligated to act in your best interest) with experience working with entrepreneurs who have gone through liquidity events. They should "Get" your values and financial philosophy, "Want" to build a long-term relationship, and have the "Capacity" (expertise, resources, platform) to manage your wealth effectively. Credentials like CFP® (Certified Financial Planner®) or CFA® (Chartered Financial Analyst®) are often good indicators of expertise.

2. **Share Your Personal Vision (Beyond the V/TO):** While your business V/TO is important context, share your personal vision for your life post-exit. What are your

dreams, fears, and family considerations? This deep understanding is crucial for them to serve you well.

3. **Full Financial Disclosure (Data):** Be completely transparent about your current financial situation, assets, liabilities, and income. This forms the basis of their planning.

4. **IDS Personal Financial Concerns:** If you have specific financial anxieties or complex family situations, treat these as Issues to be IDSed with your wealth management advisor. They can help you find solutions and build a plan that addresses them.

5. **Establish a Review Process:** Determine a regular rhythm for reviewing your financial plan, investment performance, and progress towards your goals (e.g., quarterly or semi-annually).

6. **Accountability and Traction:** While investment returns are subject to market forces, hold your advisor accountable for the quality of their advice, responsiveness, clarity of communication, and adherence to your agreed-upon investment strategy and financial plan.

INTEGRATION WITH BUSINESS EXIT PLANNING AND OTHER ADVISORS

Your wealth management advisor's work is intrinsically linked to your business exit and your other advisors.

- **M&A Advisor:** The projected net proceeds from the sale (informed by the M&A advisor's valuation and deal structure insights) are a key input into your wealth management plan.

- **Tax Advisor:** They work hand-in-hand on pre-sale tax planning, structuring the sale proceeds tax-efficiently, and managing ongoing tax liabilities from your investment portfolio.

- **Legal Advisor (Estate Planning):** Your wealth advisor coordinates with your estate planning attorney to ensure your wealth transfer goals are met through wills, trusts, and other legal instruments.

Understanding your personal financial needs *before* a sale can also influence your negotiations. If you know your "number," you're in a stronger position to evaluate offers and deal terms.

EXIT-READY ACTIONS FOR YOUR PERSONAL FINANCIAL FUTURE

Even if an exit seems distant, you can take proactive steps regarding your personal wealth management.

1. **Define preliminary post-exit goals.** Start thinking about what you want your life to look like after you're no longer running your business. What are your income needs? What are your legacy goals? Write them down.

2. **Estimate your current net worth (personal).** Get a clear picture of your personal assets and liabilities outside of the business.

3. **Review your current retirement savings and investments.** Are you maximizing your current retirement savings opportunities (e.g., 401(k), IRA)? Do you have a clear investment strategy for your personal assets?

4. **Meet with a fiduciary wealth management advisor.** Even for an initial consultation, talking to a professional can provide a valuable perspective on how to start thinking about aligning your business value with your long-term personal financial security. Ask how they typically work with business owners preparing for an exit.

5. **Discuss "what if" scenarios.** Have a preliminary conversation with your spouse or key family members about potential life changes after an exit. Getting on the same page early is beneficial.

Your wealth management advisor is your partner in translating the financial success of your business into lasting personal financial security and freedom. By engaging them early and integrating their counsel into your overall Exit Readiness strategy, you ensure that when you do transition out of your business, you are fully prepared to embrace your next chapter with confidence and peace of mind.

15

NAVIGATING THE HUMAN
SIDE OF YOUR EXIT

Exiting a business you've poured your life into is far more than just a financial transaction or a strategic maneuver. It's a profound personal transition, often laden with complex emotions, questions of identity, and the challenge of redefining purpose. While your other advisors in the Six1 Framework focus on the business, legal, financial, and transactional aspects of your exit, the Personal Coach addresses a critical, often overlooked, dimension: your personal readiness and well-being throughout this significant life change. They are your guide for the human side of the exit, helping you navigate the psychological and emotional terrain to emerge fulfilled and prepared for your next chapter.

For many entrepreneurs running on EOS, the business is deeply intertwined with their identity. The V/TO isn't just a business plan; it's a personal vision realized. The People Component isn't just an org chart; it's a team they've nurtured. The Traction isn't just progress; it's a measure of their impact. Stepping away from this can create a void, and without intentional preparation, this void can lead to feelings of loss, uncertainty, or even regret, regardless of financial success.

A Personal Coach helps you proactively address these human elements, ensuring your exit is not just profitable, but also personally rewarding.

THE ESSENTIAL ROLE OF THE PERSONAL COACH IN YOUR EXIT READINESS

A Personal Coach specializing in entrepreneurial transitions provides invaluable support by helping you:

1. **Clarify your post-exit identity.** Who are you beyond "the owner" or "the CEO"? An exit often triggers an identity shift. A coach helps you explore your values, passions, and strengths outside the context of your business, enabling you to build a fulfilling identity for your next phase of life.

2. **Develop a compelling vision for your next chapter.** Just as your V/TO guided your business, you need a personal vision for what's next. A coach facilitates this discovery process, helping you articulate what a meaningful and purposeful life after the business looks like for you. This might involve new ventures, hobbies, travel, learning, family time, or philanthropic pursuits.

3. **Navigate emotional complexities.** Selling a business can evoke a wide range of emotions: excitement, relief, sadness, anxiety, and a sense of loss. A coach provides a safe space to process these feelings, develop coping mechanisms, and maintain emotional equilibrium during a potentially stressful period.

4. **Manage relationship dynamics.** An exit can impact relationships with family, business partners, and employees. A coach can help you navigate these changes,

communicate effectively, and manage expectations, ensuring these important connections remain healthy.

5. **Redesign your life and structure.** The daily rhythm and structure provided by running a business disappear after an exit. A coach helps you intentionally design a new structure for your time, energy, and activities that aligns with your post-exit vision and prevents feelings of aimlessness.

6. **Maintain well-being.** The stress of an exit process, coupled with the uncertainty of the future, can take a toll on your physical and mental health. A coach helps you prioritize self-care, manage stress, and maintain overall well-being.

7. **Address fears and limiting beliefs.** Concerns about relevance, boredom, or financial security (even with substantial wealth) can surface. A coach helps you identify and address these underlying fears and limiting beliefs that might hinder your transition.

KEY AREAS OF FOCUS WITH YOUR PERSONAL COACH

Your work with a Personal Coach during the exit process will likely touch on several key themes.

- **Legacy:** What do you want your business legacy to be? And what personal legacy do you want to build in your next chapter?

- **Purpose:** How will you find and express your sense of purpose when you're no longer leading your company?

- **Contribution:** If making a difference is important to you, how will you continue to contribute your talents and energy?

- **Learning and Growth:** What new skills, knowledge, or experiences do you want to pursue?
- **Connection:** How will you maintain and cultivate meaningful social and professional connections?

SELECTING AND ENGAGING WITH YOUR PERSONAL COACH: AN EOS APPROACH

Choosing a Personal Coach is a very personal decision. Apply your EOS principles to find the right fit.

1. **Right Coach, Right Seat (for You):** Look for a coach with experience working with entrepreneurs, particularly those navigating major life transitions, like selling a business. Chemistry and trust are paramount. They must "Get" your unique personality and challenges, "Want" to support your personal growth, and have the "Capacity" (skills, tools, experience) to guide you effectively. Ask for testimonials or speak to former clients if possible.

2. **Share Your Personal Vision (and V/TO Context):** Be open and honest about your hopes, fears, and aspirations for your life post-exit. Sharing context about your business (perhaps a summary of your V/TO and its significance to you) can also be helpful for them to understand the magnitude of the transition.

3. **Data (Self-Reflection):** The "data" in coaching often comes from your self-reflection, journaling, and honest responses to their questions. Be prepared to do the inner work.

4. **IDS Personal Challenges:** Your coaching sessions are a place to IDS the personal obstacles, emotional hurdles,

or identity questions that arise. Your coach helps you clarify the real issue and develop strategies to solve it.

5. **Process and Rhythm:** Establish a regular coaching rhythm (e.g., bi-weekly or monthly sessions) and a clear understanding of the coaching process and expectations.

6. **Traction on Personal Goals:** While coaching is less about hard metrics, you can still gain Traction on personal development goals. This might involve committing to certain actions, exploring new activities, or practicing new mindsets between sessions.

INTEGRATING PERSONAL READINESS WITH BUSINESS EXIT PLANNING

Your personal readiness for an exit is just as important as your business's readiness. If you are not personally prepared for what comes next, even the most financially successful exit can feel hollow.

- **Timing Your Exit:** Your personal readiness can influence the timing of your business exit. If you have a clear and exciting vision for your next chapter, you may be more motivated to prepare the business for sale.

- **Negotiating Deal Terms:** Understanding your personal needs (e.g., a clean break vs. a continued role, a certain level of involvement post-sale) can inform the deal terms you are willing to accept.

- **Communicating with Stakeholders:** Being clear on your personal reasons for exiting and your plans for the future can help you communicate more effectively and authentically with your family, employees, and other stakeholders.

Your Personal Coach often works in concert, albeit sometimes indirectly, with your wealth management advisor, as your financial plan needs to support your life vision, and your life vision needs to be financially sustainable.

EXIT-READY ACTIONS FOR YOUR PERSONAL TRANSITION

To begin focusing on your personal readiness for a future exit, consider these steps.

1. **Reflect on your identity beyond the business.** Spend some time journaling or thinking about who you are, what you value, and what you enjoy, independent of your role as a business owner.

2. **Envision your ideal life post-exit.** If you sold your business tomorrow, what would you do? What would your ideal day, week, or year look like? Don't filter it yet; just dream.

3. **Talk to other exited entrepreneurs.** Seek out other business owners who have successfully transitioned out of their companies. Ask them about their personal journey, what they found challenging, and what they found fulfilling.

4. **Consider a "test drive."** If possible, start delegating more and taking small steps back from the daily grind of your business to "test drive" what more freedom or a different focus might feel like. What do you do with that extra time?

5. **Explore coaching.** Research and have initial conversations with a few Personal Coaches who specialize in working with entrepreneurs. See if their approach resonates with you.

Preparing for the human side of your exit is a profound act of self-leadership. By engaging a Personal Coach, you invest in your future well-being, ensuring that your exit is not just an end to one chapter, but a fulfilling and purposeful beginning to the next. This holistic approach to readiness is what truly defines an Exit-Ready EOS entrepreneur.

PART 3

Exit Ready Process

EXTRACT VALUE

- Due Diligence Package
- Virtual Data Room
- Confidential Info Memorandum
- Buyer Targeting Strategy
- Transaction Team Charter
- Negotiation Strategy
- Transition Management Plan

MAXIMIZE VALUE

- Exit Growth Plan
- Profitability Enhancement Strategy
- Efficiency Plan
- Management Dev. Program
- Comp. Adv. Strategy
- Rec. Rev. Model
- CX Enhancement

PROTECT VALUE

- Owner Dep. Reduction
- Governance Enhancement
- Continuity Plan
- IP Protection
- Cust. Diversification
- Risk Mitigation

PROCESSES & ADVISORS

- Advisor Team Charter
- Integrated Advisor Strategy
- Enhanced Financial Reporting System
- Operational Improvement Plan
- Market Positioning Strategy
- Advisor Scorecard

ID VALUE GAPS

- Exit Readiness Score
- Current Business Valuation
- Value Gap
- Analysis Report
- Risk Assessment Report
- Owner Dependence Evaluation
- Value Enhancement

16

UNCOVERING HIDDEN VALUE– IDENTIFYING AND CLOSING YOUR VALUE GAPS

A s an EOS-run company, you're accustomed to identifying, discussing, and solving issues to strengthen your business. The concept of a "Value Gap" in the context of Exit Readiness is similar: it's the difference between what your business is worth today and what it *could* be worth if it were fully optimized and de-risked in the eyes of a potential buyer. Identifying and systematically closing these Value Gaps is a cornerstone of the SxSE system and a critical activity in maximizing your ultimate sale price and achieving a smoother transaction.

Value Gaps aren't necessarily problems or failures; often, they are simply untapped opportunities or areas where the business hasn't yet reached its full potential from an external valuation perspective. They can exist in any aspect of your business—financial performance, operational efficiency, customer concentration, management team depth, legal preparedness, or even in how well your story is told. The key is to look at your business through the critical lens of a sophisticated buyer and proactively address any factors that might diminish its perceived value or increase perceived risk.

UNDERSTANDING VALUE GAPS: THE BUYER'S PERSPECTIVE

Buyers don't just pay for your past performance; they pay for future potential and the perceived risk associated with achieving that potential. A Value Gap, therefore, can be anything that:

- **Reduces future profitability or cash flow,** such as high customer churn, inefficient processes, or unmanaged costs.
- **Increases risk,** such as heavy owner dependence, lack of a strong management team, poor financial controls, or legal vulnerabilities.
- **Limits growth potential,** such as a narrow product line, untapped market segments, or a lack of scalability.
- **Makes the business difficult to transfer,** such as poorly documented processes, key relationships tied solely to the owner, or complex/unclear ownership structures.

By identifying these gaps well in advance of an exit, you have the runway to address them, transforming potential weaknesses into strengths and, in doing so, directly increasing the transferable value of your enterprise.

COMMON CATEGORIES OF VALUE GAPS IN EOS COMPANIES

Even well-run EOS companies can have Value Gaps when viewed through an M&A lens. Here are some common categories to consider.

1. **Owner Dependence:** Is the business overly reliant on you, the owner, for key decisions, customer relationships, or critical operational knowledge? This is a major red flag for buyers as it signifies high transition risk.

2. **Management Team Depth and Capability:** Does your leadership team (as defined on your Accountability Chart) have the proven ability to run and grow the business without you? Are there succession plans in place for key roles?

3. **Financial Performance and Reporting:** Are your financial statements clear, credible, and buyer-ready (e.g., GAAP compliant, potentially reviewed or audited)? Are there opportunities to improve revenue quality (e.g., increase recurring revenue) or enhance profit margins?

4. **Customer Concentration:** Do one or a few customers account for a disproportionately large percentage of your revenue? This creates a risk that buyers will discount.

5. **Supplier Concentration:** Similar to customer concentration, over-reliance on a single or very few suppliers can be a vulnerability.

6. **Operational Scalability:** Are your core processes (as per your Process Component) well-documented, efficient, and scalable to support future growth without significant new investment or disruption?

7. **Sales and Marketing Effectiveness:** Is your sales pipeline robust and predictable? Is your marketing strategy generating a consistent flow of qualified leads? Is your market position defensible?

8. **Legal and Compliance Issues:** Are there any unresolved legal disputes, compliance gaps, or poorly structured contracts that could create liabilities or complicate a sale?

9. **Intellectual Property (IP) Protection:** Is your valuable IP (brand, patents, software, trade secrets) adequately protected and clearly owned by the company?

10. **Lack of a Clear Growth Strategy:** While your V/TO outlines your Vision, is there a compelling and believable growth story that a buyer can invest in? Are the strategies for achieving this growth clearly articulated and validated?

APPROACHES TO ASSESSING VALUE GAPS

Identifying Value Gaps requires an objective and critical assessment of your business. Several approaches can be effective:

- **Self-Assessment Using EOS Tools:** Leverage your existing EOS disciplines. During your quarterly or annual planning, dedicate time to reviewing each of the Six Key Components through the lens of a potential buyer. Ask: "If a buyer were looking at our Vision, People, Data, Issues, Process, or Traction, what weaknesses or risks might they perceive?"

- **Engage Your Six1 Framework Advisors:** Each of your trusted advisors (legal, financial, tax, M&A, wealth, and personal coach) can help identify Value Gaps within their area of expertise. Your M&A advisor, in particular, can provide a strong market-based perspective on what buyers value and discount.

- **Formal Exit Readiness Assessment:** Consider undertaking a formal Exit Readiness Assessment, either through a specialized consultant or using a comprehensive tool (like the one provided later in this book). These assessments typically cover dozens of factors that impact business value and transferability.

- **"Mock Due Diligence":** Simulate aspects of a buyer's due diligence process. For example, have an external party review your financial statements as if they were a buyer, or try to explain your core processes to someone unfamiliar with your business.

- **Benchmarking:** Compare your company's performance on key metrics (e.g., profit margins, revenue growth, customer retention) against industry benchmarks and best-in-class companies. Significant deviations can indicate potential Value Gaps.

PRIORITIZING VALUE GAPS: IMPACT AND EFFORT

Once you've identified a list of potential Value Gaps, it's crucial to prioritize them. Not all gaps are created equal, and you can't address everything at once. A simple but effective prioritization matrix considers two factors.

1. **Potential impact on value/exit success.** How significantly would closing this gap increase your company's valuation or improve the likelihood of a smooth and successful exit?

2. **Effort/resources required to close.** How much time, money, and internal resources would be needed to address this gap effectively?

Focus your initial efforts on gaps that have a high potential impact and require a manageable level of effort (the "quick wins" or "high-leverage" items). Then, systematically address other high-impact gaps, even if they require more significant effort, by breaking them down into manageable Rocks over several quarters.

CREATING VALUE GAP CLOSURE PLANS: INTEGRATING WITH YOUR EOS TRACTION COMPONENT

Identifying Value Gaps is only the first step. The real work lies in closing them. This is where your EOS Traction Component becomes invaluable.

1. **Turn gaps into issues.** Add your prioritized Value Gaps to your company or leadership team's Issues List.
2. **IDS the gaps.** For each significant gap, utilize the IDS process to identify its root causes and generate potential solutions.
3. **Set Rocks to close gaps.** Convert the chosen solutions into specific, measurable, achievable, relevant, and time-bound (SMART) Rocks for the company or individual members of your leadership team. For example:

   - "Reduce top customer concentration from 40 percent to 25 percent by year-end."
   - "Document top 3 core operational processes by the end of Q2."
   - "Develop and implement a leadership succession plan for two key roles by Q3."

4. **Track progress in Level 10 Meetings.** Ensure these Value Gap Rocks are reviewed weekly in your Level 10 Meetings to maintain focus and accountability.

5. **Review and adjust.** Periodically (e.g., quarterly) reassess your Value Gaps. Have new ones emerged? Have priorities shifted? Have you successfully closed previously identified gaps?

THE VALUE GAP IDENTIFICATION TOOL

A practical Value Gap Identification Tool is typically structured as a comprehensive checklist or questionnaire, organized by key business areas (mirroring the Six Key Components of EOS and adding exit-specific categories, like legal and M&A readiness). For each item, the user rates their company's current status

Complete the Free Value Gap Assessment (VGA) offered by Step by Step Exit at StepbyStepExit.com/vga to begin the process.

Key Sections of a Value Gap Identification Tool include:

- **Strategic/Vision:** Clarity of V/TO, market positioning, and growth plan credibility.

- **Leadership and People:** Owner dependence, management team strength, succession planning, and employee engagement.

- **Financial Performance and Reporting:** Quality of financials, profitability trends, recurring revenue, Scorecard effectiveness, and internal controls.

- **Sales and Marketing:** Predictability of revenue, customer concentration, sales process, and brand strength.

- **Operations and Process:** Scalability, process documentation, supplier relationships, and technology utilization.

- **Legal and Compliance:** Corporate records, contract quality, IP protection, and regulatory compliance.

- **M&A Readiness:** Understanding of valuation, preparedness for due diligence, and clarity on exit objectives.

For each identified gap, the VGA provides insight and actions to close the gaps, resulting in a higher valuation of the organization. These insights feed directly into the IDS and Rock-setting process.

EXIT-READY ACTIONS FOR IDENTIFYING AND CLOSING YOUR VALUE GAPS

Begin your journey of uncovering and addressing hidden value in your company with these actions:

1. **Dedicate time for a value gap discussion.** In your next quarterly or annual strategic planning session with your leadership team, allocate specific time (e.g., 2–3 hours) to discuss potential Value Gaps from a buyer's perspective. Use the common categories listed above as a starting point.

2. **Conduct an Owner Dependence Self-Assessment.** Honestly assess how much the business relies on you. List 3–5 key functions or relationships where you are the primary person, and brainstorm who on your Accountability Chart could begin to take these over.

3. **Review your customer list for concentration.** Calculate the percentage of revenue derived from your top 5 and top 10 customers. If any single customer represents more than 15–20 percent of revenue, or your top 5 represent more than 50 percent, add "Customer Concentration" to your Issues List.

4. **Ask your advisors for input.** Schedule brief conversations with your key advisors (Financial, Legal, M&A, if you have one), and ask them: "From your perspective, what are 1–2 potential Value Gaps a buyer might see in our business?"

5. **Select one Value Gap to address as a Rock next quarter.** Based on your initial discussions, choose one manageable but impactful Value Gap and set a clear Company Rock to make progress on closing it in the next 90 days.

Identifying and closing Value Gaps is not a one-time event; it's an ongoing discipline that aligns perfectly with the EOS commitment to continuous improvement. By proactively strengthening your business from the inside out, through the critical lens of a future buyer, you not only prepare for a more lucrative and smoother exit but also build a fundamentally stronger, more resilient, and more valuable company today.

17

STRATEGIC IMPLEMENTATION— WEAVING EXIT READINESS INTO EOS

Throughout this book, we've explored the various components of becoming an Exit-Ready EOS company. We've delved into strengthening your Six Key Components, engaging your Six1 Framework of trusted advisors, and identifying and closing Value Gaps. Now, we arrive at a crucial juncture: strategic implementation. It's not enough to understand these concepts; true Exit Readiness is achieved by weaving these principles and practices into the very fabric of how you run your business using the Entrepreneurial Operating System.

Strategic implementation in this context isn't about a separate, massive project overlaid on top of your existing EOS disciplines. Instead, it's about enhancing and extending what you already do well. It's about looking at your V/TO, your Rocks, your Level 10 Meetings, your Scorecard, and your People Component through the additional lens of Exit Readiness. It's about making Exit Readiness an integrated part of your company's operating rhythm, not an afterthought or a last-minute scramble.

THE SXSE STRATEGIC IMPLEMENTATION APPROACH: LEVERAGE YOUR EOS PURITY

The Step-by-Step Exit system is designed to seamlessly integrate with EOS. The beauty of this approach is that you don't need to learn a whole new operating system. You leverage the tools and disciplines you already master, simply applying them with a heightened awareness of what makes a business attractive, valuable, and transferable to a future owner.

Key Principles of SxSE Strategic Implementation

1. **EOS First, Exit-Enhanced:** Continue to run your business on pure EOS. The Six Key Components remain your foundation. SxSE provides the strategic overlay to ensure these components are not just strong for current operations but also optimized for a future exit.

2. **Long-Term View:** Exit Readiness is not a 90-day sprint. While you'll set quarterly Rocks related to it, the most significant value creation often comes from consistent effort over several years. Think of it as a marathon, not a race.

3. **Leadership Team Alignment:** Just as with any major company initiative, your entire leadership team must be aligned on the importance of Exit Readiness and their respective roles in achieving it. This should be a regular topic in your strategic planning sessions.

4. **Advisor Integration:** Your Six1 Framework of advisors needs to be integrated into your EOS process. They should understand your V/TO, participate in relevant strategic discussions (where appropriate), and help you set and achieve Exit-Readiness Rocks.

5. **Continuous Improvement:** Exit Readiness, like EOS mastery, is a journey of continuous improvement. Regularly assess your progress, identify new Value Gaps, and adjust your plans accordingly.

INTEGRATING EXIT READINESS INTO YOUR SIX KEY COMPONENTS

When you shift to long-range thinking, time will suddenly slow down. A peace will come over you. You will start to make better decisions. You will become more consistent. You will be a better leader to your people. And the irony is that you will get to where you want to go faster.

—Gino Wickman, Author of *Traction* & *Shine*, Creator of EOS®

Let's look at how to strategically implement Exit Readiness thinking into each of the Six Key Components.

- **Vision Component**

  ○ **V/TO:** When clarifying your V/TO, explicitly discuss your long-term exit aspirations (even if they are 5–10 years out). How does your 10-Year Target align with potential exit goals? Does your 3-Year Picture include milestones that enhance transferable value (e.g., diversifying revenue, building a stronger leadership team)? Your Marketing Strategy should also consider how your brand and market position will be perceived by potential acquirers.

  ○ **Core Values and Core Focus:** Ensure these are not just internal guides, but also reflect a business that is stable, ethical, and focused—qualities attractive to buyers.

- **People Component**

  ○ **Accountability Chart:** Is your Accountability Chart structured for scalability and reduced owner dependence? Are all seats filled with the Right People in the Right Seats (RPRS) who are capable of performing their roles without your constant oversight?

  ○ **Leadership Team Development:** Actively develop your leadership team to be capable of running the business independently. This is perhaps the single most important factor in de-risking your business for a buyer.

  ○ **Succession Planning:** For key roles (including your own), have at least a conceptual succession plan. Buyers want to see continuity.

- **Data Component**

  ○ **Scorecard:** Include 2–3 key metrics on your Scorecard that directly reflect Exit Readiness or address key Value Gaps (e.g., customer concentration percentage, recurring revenue as a percent of total, owner involvement score).

  ○ **Measurables:** Ensure all employees have measurables that contribute to overall business health and value creation.

  ○ **Financial Reporting:** As discussed with your financial advisor, ensure your financial data is accurate, timely, and moving towards buyer-ready standards.

- **Issues Component**

  - **Issues List:** Regularly add Exit-Readiness items and Value Gaps to your Issues List at both the company and departmental levels.
  - **IDS:** Use the IDS process to thoroughly vet these issues and develop robust solutions. Don't just patch; solve them for the long term.

- **Process Component**

  - **Core Processes:** Ensure your 3–7 core processes are documented, simplified, and followed by all (FBA). This demonstrates operational consistency and transferability to a buyer.
  - **Scalability:** Review your processes for scalability. Can they handle significant growth without breaking?

- **Traction Component**

  - **Rocks:** Consistently set quarterly Company Rocks and Individual Rocks that are specifically aimed at closing Value Gaps or enhancing Exit Readiness.
  - **Level 10 Meetings:** Keep Exit-Readiness Rocks and related measurables visible and on track through your weekly Level 10 Meeting pulse.

THE ROLE OF YOUR SIX1 FRAMEWORK ADVISORS IN STRATEGIC IMPLEMENTATION

Your trusted advisors are not just consultants you call when there's a problem; they are integral to your strategic implementation of Exit Readiness.

- **Regular Review Cadence:** Establish a rhythm for meeting with your Six1 advisors, individually or as a group, to review progress on Exit-Readiness initiatives. This could be quarterly or semi-annually.
- **Shared Understanding of V/TO:** Ensure all your key advisors understand your company's V/TO and your personal exit objectives. This provides context for their advice.
- **Collaborative Rock Setting:** Involve your advisors in identifying potential Rocks related to their area of expertise that would enhance your Exit Readiness.
- **Accountability:** While you and your leadership team are ultimately accountable for executing, your advisors can help hold you accountable for making progress on the strategic recommendations they provide.

OVERCOMING IMPLEMENTATION CHALLENGES

Implementing Exit Readiness strategies can face challenges.

- **"It's Too Early" Mentality:** Some leaders feel it's too soon to think about exiting. Reframe Exit Readiness as building a fundamentally stronger, more valuable, and more resilient business *today*, regardless of when you sell.

- **Resource Constraints:** Addressing Value Gaps takes time and resources. Prioritize ruthlessly based on impact and use your EOS disciplines to execute efficiently.

- **Lack of Urgency:** If an exit feels distant, it's easy for Exit Readiness to fall down the priority list. Keep it visible by including relevant measurables on your Scorecard and consistently setting related Rocks.

- **Emotional Resistance:** For some owners, the thought of exiting can be emotional. Acknowledge these feelings (perhaps with the help of a Personal Coach), but don't let them derail strategic preparation.

EXIT-READY ACTIONS FOR STRATEGIC IMPLEMENTATION

To begin strategically weaving Exit Readiness into your EOS fabric:

1. **Schedule an "Exit Readiness V/TO Review."** In your next quarterly or annual planning session, dedicate a specific agenda item to review your current V/TO through the lens of Exit Readiness. Ask: "How does our current Vision support or hinder our ability to achieve an optimal exit in the future?"

2. **Identify one Exit-Readiness Measurable for your Scorecard.** Choose one key metric that reflects an important aspect of Exit Readiness for your business (e.g., percent revenue from top customer, number of core processes documented and FBA, leadership team cross-training metric) and add it to your company Scorecard.

3. **Set one Company Rock next quarter, focused on a key Value Gap.** Based on your previous Value Gap identification work, select one high-impact gap and make it a Company Rock for the upcoming quarter.

4. **Discuss Advisor Integration with your leadership team.** Have a conversation about how you can better integrate the advice and expertise of your Six1 Framework advisors into your regular EOS planning and execution rhythm.

5. **Commit to an annual Exit Readiness Review:** Make it a recurring annual agenda item to review your overall Exit Readiness progress, reassess Value Gaps, and set new priorities for the coming year.

Strategic implementation of Exit Readiness is about making small, consistent enhancements to your already strong EOS practices. By doing so, you're not just preparing for a future transaction; you're building a more robust, valuable, and ultimately, more enjoyable business to run today. You are creating a company that is not only great to own but also highly attractive to others when the time is right for you to step into your next adventure.

18

FORTIFY YOUR FORTRESS

A s you diligently work to build an Exit-Ready EOS company, systematically strengthening your Six Key Components and closing Value Gaps, it's equally crucial to protect the value you are creating. Value protection is not a passive activity; it's an ongoing, proactive effort to safeguard your company's assets, earnings power, and overall attractiveness to potential buyers from a myriad of internal and external threats. Just as a medieval fortress had strong walls, vigilant guards, and well-stocked provisions, an Exit-Ready business must have robust defenses in place to preserve its hard-won worth.

Failing to protect value can lead to significant erosion of what you've built, sometimes rapidly and unexpectedly. A key customer loss, a data breach, an unforeseen legal dispute, or the departure of a critical employee can all diminish your company's appeal and valuation. Therefore, integrating value protection strategies into your EOS disciplines is essential for ensuring that when you are ready to exit, the business is as sound and secure as possible.

THE IMPERATIVE OF VALUE PROTECTION IN EXIT READINESS

Value protection is about mitigating risks—financial, operational, legal, market-related, and human capital risks. From a buyer's perspective, a business with well-managed risks is inherently more valuable and less prone to post-acquisition surprises. Key principles of value protection include:

1. **Proactive Risk Identification:** Regularly scanning the horizon for potential threats, both internal and external.
2. **Mitigation Strategies:** Implementing specific measures to reduce the likelihood or impact of identified risks.
3. **Contingency Planning:** Having plans in place to respond effectively if a risk materializes.
4. **Building Resilience:** Creating a business that can withstand shocks and adapt to changing circumstances.

KEY STRATEGIES FOR PROTECTING YOUR BUSINESS VALUE

Value protection strategies span across all areas of your business. Here are some critical areas to focus on, many of which will involve collaboration with your Six1 Framework advisors.

1. **Legal Protections**

   o **Strong Contracts:** Ensure you have robust, well-drafted contracts with customers, suppliers, and key employees. This includes clear terms, confidentiality clauses, non-compete/non-solicit agreements (where enforceable and appropriate), and intellectual property ownership clauses.

- **Intellectual Property (IP) Safeguards:** Actively protect your trademarks, patents, copyrights, and trade secrets. This includes proper registration, clear ownership documentation, and internal policies to prevent infringement or loss.

- **Corporate Governance and Compliance:** Maintain meticulous corporate records, ensure compliance with all relevant regulations (industry-specific, labor laws, environmental, etc.), and proactively address any potential legal vulnerabilities. Your legal advisor is key here.

2. **Financial Protections**

- **Internal Controls:** Implement and maintain strong internal controls over financial reporting to prevent errors, fraud, and ensure the accuracy of your financial data. Your financial advisor can guide this.

- **Insurance Coverage:** Regularly review your business insurance policies (general liability, professional liability/E&O, D&O, cybersecurity, property, etc.) to ensure adequate coverage for your current risk profile.

- **Cash Flow Management:** Maintain healthy cash reserves and conduct diligent cash flow forecasting to weather unexpected downturns or capitalize on opportunities.

- **Credit Risk Management:** Have clear policies for extending credit to customers and managing receivables to minimize bad debt.

3. **Operational Protections**

- ○ **Cybersecurity and Data Protection:** In today's digital world, protecting your data and systems from breaches, ransomware, and other cyber threats is paramount. Implement robust cybersecurity measures and have an incident response plan.

- ○ **Business Continuity and Disaster Recovery Planning:** What happens if your facility is damaged, a key system fails, or a critical supplier is disrupted? Have documented plans to ensure operational continuity.

- ○ **Supply Chain Diversification:** Reduce reliance on single-source suppliers for critical components or services where possible.

- ○ **Quality Control:** Maintain rigorous quality control processes to protect your reputation and prevent costly product recalls or service failures.

4. **Human Capital Protections**

- ○ **Employee Retention:** High employee turnover, especially of key talent, can be a significant Value Gap. Focus on creating a strong culture (your People Component) and competitive compensation/benefits to retain your best people.

- ○ **Knowledge Transfer and Cross-Training:** Minimize "key person" risk by ensuring critical knowledge is documented (Process Component) and shared, and that multiple people are capable of performing essential functions.

- ○ **Non-Disclosure Agreements (NDAs):** Use NDAs with employees, contractors, and potential partners to protect confidential information.

- **Non-Compete Agreements (NCAs):** Use NCAs with employees, contractors, and potential buyers to restrict competitive activities for a defined time and territory—safeguarding your market position, preserving goodwill, and preventing key talent or partners from taking sensitive know-how to a rival.

5. **Customer and Market Protections**

- **Customer Diversification:** Actively work to reduce over-reliance on any single customer or small group of customers.
- **Customer Relationship Management:** Implement systems and processes to maintain strong, institutionalized relationships with key customers, not just relationships dependent on the owner or a single salesperson.
- **Reputation Management:** Monitor your brand's reputation online and offline and have strategies to address any negative sentiment proactively.
- **Competitive Monitoring:** Stay aware of competitive threats and market changes that could impact your business.

INTEGRATING VALUE PROTECTION INTO YOUR EOS RHYTHM

Value protection shouldn't be a separate initiative but rather an integrated part of your ongoing EOS execution.

- **Vision Component:** Your V/TO should implicitly consider a future state where value is protected. Your 1-Year Plan might include specific value protection goals.

- **People Component:** Assign clear accountability on your Accountability Chart for key risk management areas (e.g., cybersecurity, legal compliance, HR risk).

- **Data Component:** Include measurables on your Scorecard that track key risk indicators or the progress of value protection initiatives (e.g., customer concentration percentage, employee turnover rate, number of open legal issues).

- **Issues Component:** Potential risks and value protection gaps should be regularly added to your Issues List and IDSed to develop solutions.

- **Process Component:** Document and implement core processes related to risk management and value protection (e.g., contract review process, data backup process, new employee onboarding that includes confidentiality training).

- **Traction Component:** Set quarterly Rocks to implement specific value protection measures or to address identified vulnerabilities.

VALUE PROTECTION ASSESSMENT TOOLS

A Value Protection Assessment Tool guides you through a systematic review of potential risks and the adequacy of your current protective measures. It's organized by risk category (legal, financial, operational, Human Capital, market) and, for each specific risk, prompts you to consider:

1. **Likelihood:** How likely is this risk to occur?
2. **Potential Impact:** If it occurs, what would be the financial, operational, or reputational impact?

3. **Current Mitigation Measures:** What protections do you currently have in place?

4. **Effectiveness of Measures:** How effective are these current measures?

5. **Gaps/Further Action Needed:** What additional steps should be taken to better protect value in this area?

This assessment feeds into your Issues List and Rock-setting process, allowing you to prioritize and systematically enhance your value protection efforts. This process follows after the VGA and is available at StepbyStepExit.com/vga.

EXIT-READY ACTIONS FOR FORTIFYING YOUR VALUE

Start strengthening your company's defenses today with these actions:

1. **Conduct a "Top 5 Risks" Brainstorm.** With your leadership team, brainstorm the top 5 risks that could significantly erode your company's value if they materialize. For each, briefly discuss current mitigations and potential further actions.

2. **Review your business insurance coverage.** Schedule a meeting with your insurance broker to review all your current business insurance policies. Ensure the coverage limits and types are appropriate for your current scale and risk exposure. Ask specifically about cybersecurity insurance.

3. **Assess your contract strength.** Ask your legal advisor to review your standard customer contract and standard employment agreement (especially for key employees) to identify any weaknesses or areas for improvement in terms of protecting the company's interests.

4. **Evaluate your data backup and recovery process.** When was the last time you tested your data backup and recovery plan? Ensure it's robust and regularly tested.

5. **Add "Value Protection Review" as an annual agenda item.** Make it a recurring part of your annual strategic planning to conduct a high-level review of your key value protection measures and identify any new or evolving risks.

Protecting the value you've painstakingly built is not just good business practice; it's a fundamental requirement for achieving a successful and rewarding exit. By integrating these value protection strategies into your EOS disciplines, you build a more resilient, secure, and ultimately more valuable enterprise that is truly prepared for whatever the future holds, including a highly successful sale.

19

PEAK PERFORMANCE— ACTIVELY MAXIMIZING YOUR BUSINESS'S TRANSFERABLE VALUE

Becoming Exit-Ready isn't just about de-risking your business and ensuring it's well-prepared for a transaction; it's also about actively and strategically maximizing its transferable value. This means going beyond merely running a good company to building an *exceptional* one—an enterprise that is not only attractive to buyers but commands a premium valuation due to its superior financial performance, operational excellence, strong market position, and clear growth trajectory. Value maximization is the proactive, offensive counterpart to value protection, and it's where your EOS disciplines truly shine in creating a highly desirable asset.

While closing Value Gaps (Chapter 16) addresses deficiencies, maximizing value focuses on amplifying strengths and capitalizing on opportunities. It's about taking what's good and making it great, ensuring that every facet of your business contributes to its peak performance and, consequently, its peak worth in the M&A marketplace.

THE ESSENCE OF VALUE MAXIMIZATION: BEYOND THE BASELINE

Value maximization in the context of Exit Readiness involves a deliberate focus on the key drivers that sophisticated buyers look for and are willing to pay more for. These drivers often include:

1. **Superior Financial Performance:** Consistently strong revenue growth, high and sustainable profit margins, predictable cash flow, and a healthy balance sheet.

2. **Operational Excellence:** Highly efficient, scalable, and well-documented core processes that lead to consistent quality and cost-effectiveness.

3. **Strong and Defensible Market Position:** A clear competitive advantage, significant market share in a growing niche, a strong brand, and a loyal customer base.

4. **Identifiable Growth Opportunities:** Clear, credible, and actionable pathways for future growth that a new owner can readily pursue.

5. **High-Quality Management Team:** A capable and deep leadership team that can execute the growth plan and operate the business effectively post-acquisition, reducing reliance on the seller.

6. **Recurring Revenue Streams:** A significant portion of revenue that is predictable and contractual (e.g., subscriptions, long-term service agreements) is highly valued.

KEY STRATEGIES FOR MAXIMIZING TRANSFERABLE VALUE

Leveraging your EOS framework, you can implement several strategies to actively maximize your company's value.

1. **Enhance Financial Performance Systematically**

   o **Revenue Growth Initiatives:** Focus on your Marketing Strategy (V/TO) and sales processes to drive consistent top-line growth. Explore new markets, customer segments, or service/product extensions.

   o **Profit Margin Improvement:** Continuously analyze your cost structure (COGS and operating expenses) and identify opportunities for efficiency gains or strategic price increases. Use your Scorecard to track gross and net profit margins closely.

   o **Increase Recurring Revenue:** Actively seek ways to convert one-time sales into recurring revenue models. This significantly enhances valuation multiples.

   o **Optimize Working Capital:** Efficiently manage receivables, payables, and inventory to improve cash flow and reduce the capital tied up in operations.

2. **Develop and Showcase Operational Excellence**

   o **Process Optimization (Process Component):** Go beyond just documenting your core processes; continuously refine them for greater efficiency, quality, and scalability. Implement Lean principles or other improvement methodologies where appropriate.

   o **Technology Leverage:** Invest strategically in technology that can automate tasks, improve data analytics

(Data Component), enhance customer experience, or create operational leverage.

- o **Scalability Proof Points:** Demonstrate that your operations can handle significant growth without a proportional increase in fixed costs or complexity.

3. Strengthen Your Market Position and Brand

- o **Niche Dominance:** Aim to be a recognized leader in your specific market niche (Core Focus). A strong position in a well-defined niche is often more valuable than being a small player in a broad market.
- o **Brand Building:** Invest in your brand to enhance recognition, credibility, and customer loyalty. This includes your online presence, marketing communications, and customer experience.
- o **Competitive Differentiation:** Clearly articulate and continuously reinforce your unique selling propositions (USPs) and competitive advantages.

4. Cultivate and Demonstrate Growth Potential

- o **Develop a Compelling Growth Story:** Backed by data and a clear plan (part of your V/TO), articulate 2–3 clear avenues for significant future growth. This could include new product or service launches, geographic expansion, or strategic partnerships.
- o **Invest in Innovation:** Foster a culture of innovation that leads to new offerings or improvements that can drive future revenue streams.
- o **Strategic Acquisitions (If Applicable):** For some, small, strategic "tuck-in" acquisitions can accelerate

growth and enhance market position before a larger exit.

5. **Build an Irreplaceable (but Transferable) Leadership Team**

   ○ **Empower Your People (People Component):** Delegate effectively and empower your leadership team to take full ownership of their roles on The Accountability Chart.

   ○ **Develop Future Leaders:** Implement leadership development programs and create opportunities for high-potential employees to grow.

   ○ **Incentivize Key Talent:** Consider offering retention bonuses or phantom stock plans to key leaders that vest upon a successful sale, thereby aligning their interests with yours.

INTEGRATING VALUE MAXIMIZATION INTO YOUR EOS DISCIPLINES

Value maximization efforts should be woven into your existing EOS practices.

- **Vision Component:** Your 10-Year Target and 3-Year Picture should reflect ambitious but achievable value-maximization goals. Your Marketing Strategy should be geared towards building a premium brand and establishing a strong market position.

- **People Component:** Ensure you have the Right People in the Right Seats to drive these value-enhancing initiatives.

Performance reviews and development plans should align with building a high-caliber team.

- **Data Component:** Your Scorecard and departmental measurables should track KPIs directly related to value drivers (e.g., customer acquisition cost, lifetime value, revenue per employee, new product revenue percentage).

- **Issues Component:** Opportunities for value maximization, or obstacles to achieving it, should be treated as Issues to be IDSed.

- **Process Component:** Your core processes should be designed not just for current efficiency but also for scalability and to support your growth initiatives.

- **Traction Component:** Set aggressive but achievable quarterly Rocks that are specifically focused on executing your value maximization strategies. Review progress weekly in your Level 10 Meetings.

VALUE MAXIMIZATION OPPORTUNITY ASSESSMENT

Value Maximization Opportunity Assessments help you and your leadership team brainstorm and prioritize initiatives that significantly boost your company's transferable value. It involves:

1. **Financial Upside:** What are the 2–3 biggest opportunities to improve revenue growth or profitability in the next 12–24 months?

2. **Operational Leverage:** Where can we gain the most significant operational efficiencies or scalability improvements?

3. **Market Expansion/Penetration:** What untapped customer segments, geographic areas, or product/service adjacencies offer the best growth potential?

4. **Strategic Moat:** How can we further strengthen our competitive advantages and make our market position more defensible?

5. **Team Enhancement:** What's the single most impactful investment we can make in our leadership team's capability or depth?

For each identified opportunity, you assess its potential impact on value, the resources required, and the timeline for execution, feeding this into your strategic planning and Rock-setting process. Start the process by completing the VGA at StepbyStepExit.com/vga.

EXIT-READY ACTIONS FOR ACTIVELY MAXIMIZING YOUR VALUE

Embark on your value maximization journey with these focused actions.

1. **Dedicate a strategic session to value maximization.** In your next quarterly or annual planning meeting, allocate time specifically to brainstorm and prioritize 2–3 key initiatives aimed at significantly increasing transferable value over the next 12–18 months.

2. **Analyze your revenue quality.** Review your revenue streams. What percentage is recurring or contractual? Set a Rock to explore opportunities to increase this percentage.

3. **Identify one key process for scalability improvement.** Choose one of your core processes that is critical for growth and set a Rock to improve its efficiency and scalability.

4. **"Blue Sky" growth opportunities.** With your leadership team, conduct a "blue sky" brainstorming session on new growth avenues (new markets, products, services, channels). Select the most promising one for further investigation as a potential Rock.

5. **Review your leadership team's "Bus Factor."** For each key leader (including yourself), ask: "If this person were hit by a bus tomorrow, how significantly would it impact the business?" Identify areas where cross-training or succession planning needs to be a priority.

Actively maximizing your business's value is the pinnacle of Exit Readiness. It's about transforming your company from a well-run operation into a premium asset that commands top dollar and attracts the best buyers. By strategically leveraging your EOS disciplines to enhance financial performance, operational excellence, market position, and growth potential, you are not just preparing for an exit; you are building a legacy of peak performance.

20

EXTRACTING VALUE FROM YOUR EXIT-READY BUSINESS

After years of diligently running your company on EOS, strengthening its Six Key Components, engaging your Six1 Framework of advisors, and systematically building an Exit-Ready enterprise, the time eventually comes to reap the rewards of your hard work: extracting the value you've created. This is the culmination of your journey, the point where strategic preparation meets market opportunity. Extracting maximum value isn't just about finding a buyer; it's about orchestrating a well-planned transaction process that aligns with your personal and financial goals and leverages the inherent strengths of your Exit-Ready business.

This chapter focuses on the practical strategies and principles for navigating the actual sale process. It's where your M&A advisor takes a leading role, but your understanding of the process, your preparedness, and the active involvement of your entire leadership team and other key advisors remain crucial for success. An Exit-Ready business enters this phase from a position of strength, clarity, and control, rather than reacting to unsolicited offers or market pressures.

THE ESSENCE OF STRATEGIC VALUE EXTRACTION

Strategic Value Extraction is about more than just achieving the highest possible price. While price is a critical component, a truly successful exit also considers:

1. **Optimal deal structure.** The terms of the deal (cash vs. stock, earnouts, seller financing, tax implications) can be as important as the headline number.

2. **Alignment with personal goals.** Does the exit allow you to achieve your desired lifestyle, legacy, and future pursuits? (Refer back to your work with your wealth management and Personal Coach).

3. **Favorable terms and minimized risk.** Negotiating strong representations, warranties, and indemnification clauses to protect you from post-closing liabilities.

4. **A smooth and efficient process.** A well-prepared company experiences a less disruptive and faster due diligence and closing process.

5. **Finding the right buyer.** Beyond price, is the buyer a good cultural fit (if you care about legacy or employee continuity)? Do they have the resources to take the business to the next level?

KEY PRINCIPLES FOR EXTRACTING VALUE

- **Preparation is Paramount:** The more prepared your business is (financially, operationally, and legally), the stronger your negotiating position and the smoother the transaction will be.

- **Create Competitive Tension:** The best way to maximize price and terms is to have multiple qualified buyers interested in your business.

- **Maintain Confidentiality:** Protect sensitive information throughout the process to avoid disrupting your business or compromising your negotiating leverage.

- **Control the Narrative:** Proactively present your company's story, strengths, and growth opportunities in the best possible light.

- **Be Patient but Decisive:** The sale process can take time. Be patient through the steps, but be ready to make key decisions when needed.

KEY STRATEGIES FOR SUCCESSFUL VALUE EXTRACTION

Working closely with your M&A advisor and other members of your Six1 Framework, you'll employ several key strategies.

1. **Selecting the Optimal Exit Option**

   o Revisit the various exit paths (strategic sale, private equity, MBO, ESOP, etc.) with your M&A advisor. Based on your current business status, market conditions, and personal goals, confirm which option is the best fit.

   o Understand the typical valuation ranges and deal structures associated with your chosen path.

2. **Thorough Transaction Preparation**

   o **Assemble Your Deal Team:** Ensure your M&A advisor, legal advisor (with M&A experience), tax advisor, and financial advisor (or internal finance leader) are ready and coordinated.

○ **Prepare a Professional Confidential Information Memorandum (CIM):** This comprehensive document, typically prepared by your M&A advisor, is your company's marketing brochure for potential buyers. It should highlight your history, strengths, V/TO summary, financial performance, management team, and growth opportunities.

○ **Organize Your Data Room:** Proactively gather and organize all the documents a buyer will request during due diligence (financials, contracts, legal documents, HR information, etc.) in a secure virtual data room. An Exit-Ready company has much of this already well-organized.

○ **Anticipate Due Diligence Questions:** Think like a buyer. What questions would you ask? What are your potential weaknesses? Prepare honest and well-supported answers.

3. **Executing a Strategic Go-to-Market Process**

○ **Targeted Buyer Identification:** Your M&A advisor will develop a list of qualified potential buyers (strategic and/or financial) who are most likely to see value in your company and have the capacity to transact.

○ **Confidential Outreach:** The M&A advisor will manage the initial confidential outreach to these potential buyers, typically starting with a blind teaser and then, under NDA, providing the CIM.

- Managing Buyer Interactions: They will coordinate management presentations, site visits, and Q&A sessions with interested parties.

4. Mastering Negotiation Strategy

- Soliciting Indications of Interest (IOIs) and Letters of Intent (LOIs): Your M&A advisor will manage the process of receiving initial non-binding offers (IOIs) and then more detailed LOIs from the most serious contenders. The goal is to create a competitive environment.

- Negotiating Key Terms: Beyond price, focus on negotiating critical terms in the LOI, such as form of consideration, exclusivity period, due diligence scope, working capital targets, and key conditions to closing. Your legal and tax advisors will be heavily involved here.

- Maintaining Leverage: Even after selecting a primary buyer and signing an LOI, maintain a professional relationship with other interested parties if possible, as this can provide leverage if the primary deal encounters issues.

5. Navigating Due Diligence and Closing

- Facilitating Due Diligence: Respond promptly and thoroughly to the buyer's due diligence requests. Your organized data room will be invaluable.

- Negotiating the Definitive Purchase Agreement (DPA): This is the final legal agreement. Your legal advisor will lead these complex negotiations, focusing on representations, warranties, indemnities, and closing conditions.

- ○ **Closing the Deal:** Work through the final steps to satisfy all closing conditions and legally transfer ownership.

TRANSACTION READINESS ASSESSMENT TOOLS

Transaction Readiness Assessment Tools help you and your deal team evaluate your preparedness for the intense scrutiny of a sale process. It covers areas such as:

1. **Financial Data Integrity:** Are your historical financials accurate, complete, and readily auditable? Are your forecasts well-supported?
2. **Legal & Corporate Structure:** Are all corporate records in order? Are there any outstanding legal issues? Is your ownership structure clear?
3. **Contractual Commitments:** Are all key customer, supplier, and employment contracts organized and favorable?
4. **Operational Transparency:** Can your operations and processes be easily understood and verified by a buyer?
5. **Management Team Preparedness:** Is your leadership team prepared for buyer presentations and due diligence Q&A?
6. **Data Room Readiness:** Have you identified and started to gather the key documents for a virtual data room?

This assessment helps identify any last-minute items that need to be addressed before actively going to market, minimizing surprises and delays during the actual transaction. Start the process by completing the VGA at StepbyStepExit. com/vga.

INTEGRATING VALUE EXTRACTION WITH YOUR EOS DISCIPLINES

Even during the active sale process, your EOS disciplines remain relevant:

- **Vision & Data:** Your V/TO and historical data form the core of your CIM and buyer presentations. Clarity and credibility are key.
- **People:** Your leadership team will be heavily involved in management presentations and due diligence. Their professionalism and competence are on display.
- **Issues:** The sale process will inevitably generate Issues (e.g., tough negotiation points, unexpected due diligence findings). Use IDS with your deal team to address them effectively.
- **Process:** Having a clear internal process for managing due diligence requests and responding to the buyer is crucial.
- **Traction:** Maintaining focus and momentum throughout the often lengthy sales process requires Traction. Your M&A advisor helps drive this, but your internal commitment is also vital.

EXIT-READY ACTIONS FOR PREPARING TO EXTRACT VALUE

As you approach the point of actively considering a sale, take these preparatory actions.

1. **Select your M&A advisor (if not already done).** This is a critical first step. Ensure they are the Right Person in the Right Seat for your company and exit goals.

2. **Conduct a Preliminary Transaction Readiness Assessment.** Use a checklist (or the conceptual tool above) to identify any gaps in your preparedness for a sales process.

3. **Develop a Preliminary Data Room Index.** Start outlining the categories of documents you will need for a virtual data room and identify where they are located.

4. **Role-play management presentations.** Practice presenting your company's story and financial performance as if you were presenting to potential buyers. Get feedback from your leadership team and advisors.

5. **Align with your leadership team on the process.** Ensure your key leaders understand the stages of the sale process, the importance of confidentiality, and their potential roles.

Extracting value from your Exit-Ready business is the final, critical phase of your entrepreneurial journey with this company. By approaching it with the same strategic discipline, preparation, and teamwork that you applied to building the business through EOS, you significantly increase your chances of achieving a transaction that not only rewards you financially but also allows you to transition to your next chapter with confidence and a sense of accomplishment.

21

LIFE AFTER EXIT

Selling your business is a monumental achievement, often the culmination of a lifetime's work. The transaction closes, the funds arrive, and suddenly, the daily rhythm of running your EOS company is replaced by a new reality. This new reality is filled with immense opportunity but also requires a different kind of strategic thinking—managing your newfound wealth effectively and, just as importantly, crafting a fulfilling life beyond the business you've poured your heart and soul into. This chapter, building on the groundwork laid with your wealth management advisor and Personal Coach, focuses on the principles and practices for thriving in your post-exit world.

Many entrepreneurs are so focused on the exit event itself that they give little thought to what comes after. Yet, this next chapter can be just as challenging and rewarding as building the business, provided you approach it with the same intentionality and strategic foresight you applied using EOS. It's about shifting from value creation *within* a business to value creation *in your life*, leveraging your financial resources and personal passions to design a future that is both secure and deeply meaningful.

THE DUAL PILLARS OF POST-EXIT SUCCESS: WEALTH STEWARDSHIP AND LIFE DESIGN

Successfully navigating life after selling your business rests on two interconnected pillars.

1. **Prudent Wealth Stewardship:** This involves more than just investing your sale proceeds. It's about developing a comprehensive strategy to protect, grow, and utilize your wealth in alignment with your long-term financial goals, risk tolerance, and legacy aspirations. It requires ongoing discipline, education, and a strong partnership with your wealth management advisor.

2. **Intentional Life Design:** With the demands of business ownership lifted, you have a unique opportunity to redefine your purpose, explore new interests, and structure your time around what truly matters to you. This involves introspection, planning, and a willingness to embrace new identities and experiences, often guided by your Personal Coach.

Neglecting either of these pillars can lead to dissatisfaction. Financial security without purpose can feel empty, while pursuing passions without a sound financial footing can create stress.

KEY PRINCIPLES FOR MANAGING YOUR WEALTH POST-EXIT

Your wealth management advisor will be your primary guide here, but understanding these core principles will empower you to be an active and informed steward of your capital.

1. **Develop a comprehensive financial plan.** This is your personal V/TO for your wealth. It should outline your income needs, spending plans, investment objectives, risk tolerance, estate planning goals, and philanthropic intentions. It's a living document that should be reviewed and updated regularly.

2. **Prioritize capital preservation, then growth.** Especially in the initial period after a sale, protecting your principal is paramount. Once your core financial security is established, you can then consider strategies for growth, always balanced against your risk tolerance.

3. **Diversification is key.** Avoid concentrating your wealth in too few assets or asset classes. A well-diversified portfolio helps mitigate risk and can provide more consistent returns over time.

4. **Understand your investment time horizon.** Are you investing for short-term income, medium-term goals, or long-term legacy? Your time horizon significantly influences your investment strategy.

5. **Manage for tax efficiency.** Work with your wealth and tax advisors to structure your investments and withdrawals in a way that minimizes your tax burden legally and effectively.

6. **Plan for inflation and longevity.** Ensure your financial plan accounts for the eroding effects of inflation over time and the possibility of a long lifespan. You need your wealth to last.

7. **Regularly review and rebalance.** Your financial plan and investment portfolio are not "set it and forget it." Market conditions change, and so do your personal circumstances. Regular reviews and rebalancing are essential.

CRAFTING YOUR FULFILLING LIFE POST-EXIT: THE LIFESTYLE DEVELOPMENT FRAMEWORK

Beyond the financials, how do you build a rich and rewarding life after the intensity of entrepreneurship? Consider these elements, often explored with your Personal Coach.

1. **Redefine Your Identity and Purpose**

    o Who are you now that you're not "the boss"? Explore other facets of your identity—spouse, parent, mentor, learner, adventurer, philanthropist.

    o What gives you a sense of purpose? This might be mentoring other entrepreneurs, engaging in community work, pursuing a long-held passion project, or dedicating more time to family.

2. **Structure Your Time Meaningfully**

    o The lack of a business schedule can be disorienting. Create a new rhythm that incorporates activities you value, such as learning, health and wellness, social connections, hobbies, and relaxation.

    o Avoid the trap of over-scheduling or, conversely, drifting without focus. Find a balance that feels energizing.

3. **Nurture Relationships**

    o Invest time in strengthening relationships with family and friends, relationships that may have taken a backseat during your intense business-building years.

- ○ Seek out new communities or networks that align with your current interests.

4. **Prioritize Health and Well-Being**

- ○ Use your newfound flexibility to focus on your physical and mental health—exercise, nutrition, stress management, and adequate rest.

5. **Embrace Lifelong Learning and Growth**

- ○ What have you always wanted to learn or do? Take a course, learn a new skill, travel to new places. Keep your mind active and engaged.

6. **Consider Your Legacy and Contribution**

- ○ How do you want to make a difference in this next chapter? This could be through philanthropy, volunteering your expertise, or investing in ventures you believe in.

POST-EXIT FULFILLMENT FRAMEWORKS

Post-Exit Fulfillment Frameworks are often personal planning tools, developed with your personal coach, to help you design your next chapter. It involves defining your vision and setting goals across several key life dimensions.

- **Financial Well-being:** Goals for wealth preservation, income, legacy—linked to your financial plan
- **Health & Vitality:** Goals for physical fitness, mental well-being, energy levels

- **Relationships & Connection:** Goals for family, friends, and community involvement
- **Learning & Personal Growth:** Goals for new skills, knowledge, experiences
- **Purpose & Contribution:** Goals for making a difference, mentoring, philanthropy, and new ventures
- **Leisure & Enjoyment:** Goals for hobbies, travel, relaxation, fun

For each dimension, you articulate your desired outcomes, key activities, and perhaps even some Rocks or quarterly personal objectives to ensure you are making progress toward this fulfilling vision. The *10 Disciplines* by Gino Wickman and Rob Dube is included as a bonus chapter at the end of this book.

INTEGRATING POST-EXIT PLANNING WITH YOUR EOS MINDSET

While you're no longer running an EOS company, the disciplines you've mastered can still serve you well.

- **Vision:** Have a clear vision for your personal life, just as you had for your business (V/TO).
- **People:** Surround yourself with the right people—trusted advisors, supportive family and friends, and inspiring peers.
- **Data:** Track what matters for your personal goals (e.g., financial metrics, health indicators, progress on learning objectives).

- **Issues:** When personal challenges or dilemmas arise, IDS them: identify the real issue, discuss options, and decide on a solution.

- **Process:** Create personal processes or routines that support your well-being and goals (e.g., a morning routine, a weekly planning session for personal activities).

- **Traction:** Set personal goals (like Rocks) and hold yourself accountable for achieving them to gain traction on your new life vision.

EXIT-READY ACTIONS FOR YOUR LIFE BEYOND BUSINESS

Even before your exit, you can begin laying the groundwork for a successful transition.

1. **Start "What's Next?" conversations early.** Begin discussing your post-exit aspirations with your spouse/partner and perhaps your Personal Coach well in advance of a sale. Don't wait until the deal is done.

2. **Identify 1–2 non-business passions.** What are 1–2 interests or hobbies you'd like to dedicate more time to post-exit? Start exploring them now, even in a small way.

3. **Review your personal financial literacy.** Take some time to enhance your understanding of personal finance and investment principles. This will make you a more effective partner to your wealth management advisor.

4. **Network with exited entrepreneurs about "life after."** Seek out others who have sold their businesses and ask them about their experiences—what worked, what didn't, what they wish they'd known about crafting their next chapter.

5. **Draft a Preliminary "Post-Exit Fulfillment Framework."** Using the dimensions above (financial, health, relationships, learning, purpose, leisure), jot down some initial thoughts and goals for your life after the business.

Successfully exiting your business is a remarkable milestone. By applying strategic thought to both managing your wealth and designing your life, you can ensure that this milestone becomes a gateway to an equally rewarding and fulfilling next chapter. Your EOS journey equipped you with powerful tools for building a great business; now, adapt those tools to build a great life beyond it.

22

KNOW THYSELF—
THE EXIT READINESS ASSESSMENT

Throughout this journey of transforming your EOS-run company into an Exit-Ready enterprise, we've explored a multitude of concepts, tools, and strategies. From strengthening your Six Key Components and engaging your Six1 Framework of advisors to identifying Value Gaps, protecting value, and maximizing it, the path to Exit Readiness is comprehensive. But how do you know where you truly stand? How do you measure your progress and pinpoint the areas that require the most urgent attention? The answer lies in a thorough and honest Exit Readiness Assessment.

This chapter is dedicated to understanding the importance of self-assessment in your Exit Readiness journey. It's about taking a clear, objective look at your business through the lens of a potential buyer and the best practices we've discussed. A well-conducted assessment provides you with a baseline, highlights your strengths and weaknesses, and helps you prioritize your efforts to become truly Exit-Ready. It's the EOS discipline of Data Component applied specifically to your preparedness for an optimal exit.

THE POWER OF OBJECTIVE SELF-ASSESSMENT

As an entrepreneur who has built a business, it's easy to have blind spots or to be emotionally attached to certain aspects of your company. An objective Exit Readiness Assessment helps cut through these biases. Its power lies in:

1. **Providing a baseline.** It gives you a clear snapshot of your current state of Exit Readiness across all critical dimensions.

2. **Identifying strengths to leverage.** It highlights what you're already doing well, areas that can be showcased to potential buyers.

3. **Pinpointing critical Value Gaps and risks.** It uncovers the specific areas where your business falls short of being Exit-Ready, allowing you to focus your improvement efforts.

4. **Facilitating prioritization.** Not all gaps are created equal. An assessment helps you determine which areas will have the biggest impact on your valuation and transferability if addressed.

5. **Creating a Roadmap for Improvement.** The results of the assessment become the foundation for your Exit Readiness Rocks and longer-term strategic initiatives.

6. **Tracking progress over time.** By conducting assessments periodically (e.g., annually), you can measure your improvement and ensure you're staying on track with your Exit Readiness goals.

HOW TO ASSESS YOUR CURRENT EXIT READINESS: KEY AREAS OF FOCUS

An effective Exit Readiness Assessment should be comprehensive, covering all the facets of your business that a sophisticated buyer will scrutinize. Drawing from the SxSE Model and the principles discussed throughout this book, key areas of assessment include:

1. **Strength of Your Six Key Components (EOS Purity & Exit Enhancement)**

   o **Vision:** Clarity of V/TO, strength of Core Values and Core Focus, market understanding, and a compelling growth story.

   o **People:** RPRS in all seats on The Accountability Chart, leadership team depth and capability, owner dependence level, and succession planning.

   o **Data:** Robust Scorecard with leading indicators, accurate and timely financial reporting, and a data-driven decision-making culture.

   o **Issues:** Effectiveness of IDS at all levels, open and honest culture, and proactive problem-solving.

   o **Process:** Core processes documented, simplified, and FBA; and operational efficiency and scalability.

   o **Traction:** Consistent Rock completion, effective Level 10 Meetings, overall accountability, and execution discipline.

2. **Effectiveness of Your Six1 Framework of Advisors**

   ○ Are all six advisor roles filled with competent professionals who understand your business and exit goals?

   ○ How well are they integrated into your strategic planning and execution?

   ○ Is their advice being actively implemented?

3. **Value Gap Status**

   ○ Have you identified your key Value Gaps (financial, operational, market, people, legal)?

   ○ Do you have clear plans in place to close these gaps?

   ○ What progress has been made?

4. **Value Protection Measures**

   ○ Strength of legal protections (contracts, IP, compliance).

   ○ Robustness of financial controls and insurance.

   ○ Effectiveness of operational safeguards (cybersecurity, business continuity).

   ○ Human capital retention and knowledge transfer strategies.

5. **Value Maximization Initiatives**

   ○ Clarity and execution of strategies to enhance financial performance (revenue growth, margin improvement, recurring revenue).

   ○ Progress on developing operational excellence and scalability.

- ○ Strength of market position, brand, and competitive differentiation.
- ○ Credibility of identified growth opportunities.

6. **Transaction Readiness**

- ○ Quality and organization of financial records and legal documentation.
- ○ Preparedness of the management team for due diligence and buyer interactions.
- ○ Understanding of the M&A process and potential exit options.

7. **Personal and Financial Preparedness of the Owner(s)**

- ○ Clarity on personal post-exit goals (financial and lifestyle).
- ○ Adequacy of personal financial planning and wealth management strategy.
- ○ Emotional readiness for the transition.

THE EXIT READINESS ASSESSMENT TOOLS

Exit Readiness Assessment Tools take the form of detailed questionnaires or scorecards. A tool is available at ExitFocused. com/tools.

KEY FEATURES OF A GOOD ASSESSMENT TOOL

- • **Comprehensive Coverage:** Ensures all critical aspects of Exit Readiness are evaluated.

- **Objective Criteria:** Provides clear definitions or examples for each rating level to minimize subjectivity.

- **Action-Oriented:** The questions should naturally lead to identifying areas for improvement.

- **Scoring Mechanism:** Allows for a quantitative summary of your current readiness level, perhaps with an overall score and sub-scores for key categories.

- **Prioritization Framework:** May include a way to weigh the importance of different areas based on your specific business and exit goals.

INTERPRETING YOUR RESULTS

Once the assessment is complete, the next step is to analyze the results:

- **Overall Score:** Gives you a general sense of your current Exit Readiness.

- **Category Scores:** Highlight which broad areas (e.g., People Component, Value Protection) are your strongest and weakest.

- **Specific Low Scores:** Pinpoint the individual items or questions where you rated poorly—these are your immediate areas for attention.

IDENTIFYING PRIORITY AREAS FOR IMPROVEMENT

Don't try to fix everything at once. Based on your assessment results, work with your leadership team and advisors to prioritize the 2–3 areas that will have the most significant positive impact on your Exit Readiness if addressed. These become candidates for your next set of Company Rocks.

CREATING YOUR EXIT READINESS BASELINE AND SETTING GOALS

Your first comprehensive assessment establishes your baseline. From this baseline, you can set realistic and measurable Exit Readiness goals for the next 6–12 months. For example, "Improve our Process Component score from 3 to 4 by documenting and implementing two more core processes."

TRACKING PROGRESS OVER TIME

Re-take the assessment periodically (e.g., annually or semi-annually) to track your progress against your baseline and goals. This creates a cycle of continuous improvement, much like your regular EOS check-ups.

EXIT-READY ACTIONS FOR ASSESSING YOUR PREPAREDNESS

Begin the crucial process of self-assessment with these steps:

1. **Schedule an "Exit Readiness Assessment" session.** Dedicate a specific meeting (perhaps a half-day) with your leadership team to conduct an initial, high-level Exit Readiness Assessment. You can create a simple version based on the key areas outlined in this chapter.

2. **Engage an external facilitator (optional but recommended).** Consider having an experienced Exit Planning Advisor or M&A advisor facilitate your first comprehensive assessment. Their objectivity and expertise can be invaluable.

3. **Be brutally honest.** Encourage a culture of open and honest feedback during the assessment. The goal is to identify real weaknesses, not to make everyone feel good.

4. **Identify your top 3–5 improvement priorities.** Based on your initial assessment, what are the 3–5 most critical areas you need to work on to improve your Exit Readiness? Add these to your company's Issues List for IDS.

5. **Commit to an annual reassessment.** Make the Exit Readiness Assessment a recurring annual discipline to ensure continuous focus and improvement on your journey to an optimal exit.

Knowing where you stand is the first step to getting where you want to go. A thorough Exit Readiness Assessment, conducted with honesty and objectivity, provides the clarity and focus needed to transform your EOS-run company into a highly valuable and transferable asset, fully prepared for a successful exit when the time is right.

23

HITTING THE GROUND RUNNING—YOUR FIRST 90 DAYS TO EXIT READINESS

The journey to becoming an Exit-Ready EOS company can seem daunting at first glance. We've covered a vast landscape, from the foundational Six Key Components to the intricacies of Value Gaps, advisor frameworks, and ultimately, the sale process itself. But like any great endeavor, it begins with the first few steps. This chapter is designed to provide a clear, actionable roadmap for your first 90 days. It's about building initial momentum, securing quick wins, and establishing the rhythm that will carry you forward on your path to an optimal exit.

Think of these first 90 days as laying the critical groundwork. It's not about achieving complete Exit Readiness in three months—that's a longer-term process. Instead, it's about establishing the mindset, engaging the right people, identifying initial priorities, and integrating Exit Readiness thinking into your existing EOS disciplines. Success in these initial stages will create a powerful flywheel effect, making subsequent efforts easier and more impactful.

THE MINDSET FOR A STRONG START: CLARITY, COMMITMENT, COMMUNICATION

Before diving into specific actions, ensure you and your leadership team approach these first 90 days with the right mindset.

1. **Clarity of Purpose:** Be crystal clear on *why* Exit Readiness is important for your business and you personally. Revisit your personal and business goals. This clarity will fuel your efforts.

2. **Unwavering Commitment:** Like any significant change initiative, there will be challenges and competing priorities. Commit as a leadership team to making Exit Readiness a consistent focus.

3. **Open Communication:** Keep your leadership team informed and engaged. Explain the "why" behind these new initiatives and their role in the process. Transparency builds buy-in.

KEY OBJECTIVES FOR YOUR FIRST 90 DAYS

Your primary objectives for this initial period should be to:

- **Educate and align your leadership team.** Ensure everyone understands the core concepts of Exit Readiness and the SxSE Model.

- **Assemble your initial advisor team.** Identify and engage the first few key advisors from your Six1 Framework.

- **Conduct an Initial High-Level Assessment.** Get a preliminary understanding of your current strengths and weaknesses regarding Exit Readiness.

- **Identify and achieve 1–2 quick wins.** Secure some early successes to build confidence and demonstrate progress.
- **Integrate Exit Readiness into your EOS rhythm.** Begin incorporating Exit Readiness considerations into your V/TO, Rocks, Scorecard, and Level 10 Meetings.

YOUR 90-DAY ACTION PLAN: A WEEK-BY-WEEK GUIDE

While every company's situation is unique, here's a conceptual guide to structure your first 90 days:

WEEKS 1–2: FOUNDATION AND EDUCATION

- **Action 1: Leadership team kick-off meeting.** Dedicate a specific meeting (2–3 hours) to introducing the concept of Exit Readiness and the SxSE Model. Discuss this book's key takeaways. Share your personal commitment and the "why" behind this focus.
- **Action 2: Identify your initial "must-have" advisors.** Based on your immediate needs (often legal, financial, and M&A/Exit Planning), identify the first 2–3 advisors you need to engage or re-engage with a specific Exit Readiness focus.
- **Action 3: Schedule initial advisor consultations.** Reach out to these identified advisors, explain your new focus on Exit Readiness, and schedule initial consultations to discuss their role and how they can help.

WEEKS 3-4: INITIAL ASSESSMENT AND ADVISOR ENGAGEMENT

- **Action 4: Conduct a high-level "SWOT" for Exit Readiness.** With your leadership team, perform a simple Strengths, Weaknesses, Opportunities, and Threats analysis specifically related to your company's current Exit Readiness. This is a precursor to a more formal assessment (Chapter 22).

- **Action 5: Hold initial meetings with key advisors.** Discuss your SWOT findings and your overall Exit Readiness goals with your chosen legal, financial, and M&A/Exit Planning advisors. Get their initial perspectives on your priorities.

- **Action 6: Educate your leadership team on the Six1 Framework.** Ensure they understand the roles of each of the six key advisors and how they will contribute to the Exit Readiness journey.

WEEKS 5-8: IDENTIFYING QUICK WINS AND SETTING INITIAL ROCKS

- **Action 7: Brainstorm potential "quick win" Rocks.** Based on your SWOT and advisor feedback, identify 1-2 Rocks that are achievable within the next 90 days and will make a tangible improvement in an area of Exit Readiness (e.g., "Document one core process," "Improve one key Scorecard measurable related to financial clarity," "Review and update standard customer contract").

- **Action 8: Set your first Exit Readiness Rocks.** Formally assign these Rocks to individuals on your leadership team, with clear measurables and deadlines, just like any other Company Rock.

- **Action 9: Review your V/TO through an Exit Lens.** In a leadership team meeting, briefly review your current V/TO. Ask: "Are there any immediate, obvious disconnects between our current Vision and what would make us more Exit-Ready?" (e.g., owner dependence not addressed in 1-Year Plan).

WEEKS 9-12: BUILDING RHYTHM AND COMMUNICATING PROGRESS

- **Action 10: Integrate Exit Readiness into Level 10 Meetings.** Ensure your Exit Readiness Rocks are being tracked weekly. Add any relevant measurables to your Scorecard.

- **Action 11: Communicate progress to the wider team (as appropriate).** Depending on your company culture, share high-level progress on Exit Readiness initiatives with your broader team to build awareness and engagement.

- **Action 12: Plan your first formal Exit Readiness Assessment.** Schedule the session for your first comprehensive assessment (as detailed in Chapter 22) to occur shortly after these first 90 days. This will build on the initial momentum.

- **Action 13: Review and refine your advisor engagement.** Based on the first 90 days, are your initial advisors the Right People in the Right Seats? Are the communication and collaboration working effectively?

QUICK WINS TO IMPROVE EXIT READINESS IN THE FIRST 90 DAYS

Focusing on achievable quick wins can build significant momentum. Consider these areas:

- **Improve financial clarity.** Ensure your monthly financial statements are accurate and timely. Start tracking 1-2 new KPIs on your Scorecard that a buyer would care about (e.g., customer concentration, gross margin by product/service).

- **Document one core process.** Choose one of your most critical core processes and get it documented and followed by all (FBA). This demonstrates operational discipline.

- **Strengthen one key contract:** Review and update your standard customer agreement or a key supplier agreement with the help of your legal advisor.

- **Reduce owner dependence in one area.** Identify one key task or responsibility that only the owner currently handles and delegate it (with proper training and support) to another team member.

- **Organize your corporate records.** Ensure your basic corporate documents (formation documents, shareholder agreements, meeting minutes) are organized and readily accessible.

ESTABLISHING YOUR EXIT READINESS RHYTHM

Beyond specific actions, the goal of the first 90 days is to establish a *rhythm* of focusing on Exit Readiness. This means:

- **Regularly Discussing It:** Making Exit Readiness a recurring agenda item in leadership team meetings.

- **Consistently Setting Related Rocks:** Ensuring that each quarter includes Rocks that move you closer to your Exit Readiness goals.

- **Tracking Progress on Your Scorecard:** Having key Exit Readiness measurables visible to the leadership team weekly.

- **Involving Your Advisors Strategically:** Building a cadence of communication and collaboration with your Six1 Framework.

EXIT-READY ACTIONS FOR YOUR FIRST 90 DAYS

To kickstart your journey, commit to these actions immediately.

1. **Schedule the "Leadership Team Kick-off Meeting" for Exit Readiness** within the next two weeks.

2. **Identify and list your top 2–3 "must-have" advisors** from the Six1 Framework and assign someone to schedule initial consultations.

3. **Block out time for a "High-Level SWOT for Exit Readiness"** with your leadership team in weeks 3 or 4.

4. **Challenge your leadership team to identify one "Quick Win" Rock** related to Exit Readiness that can be accomplished in the next 90 days.

5. **Add "Exit Readiness Update" as a recurring agenda item** to your weekly Level 10 Meeting to track progress on these initial actions and Rocks.

Your first 90 days on the path to Exit Readiness are about building a solid foundation and creating momentum. By focusing on education, alignment, initial assessment, quick wins, and integrating this thinking into your EOS rhythm, you'll set your company on a clear trajectory towards achieving an optimal and rewarding exit when the time is right.

24

COMMON OBSTACLES TO EXIT READINESS AND THEIR SOLUTIONS

T he path to transforming your EOS-run company into a truly Exit-Ready enterprise is rewarding, but it's rarely without its challenges. Along the way, entrepreneurs often encounter common obstacles that can slow progress, create frustration, or even derail their efforts if not addressed proactively. Forewarned is forearmed. By understanding these typical hurdles and equipping yourself with proven solutions, you can navigate this labyrinth with greater confidence and ensure you stay on track to achieve your optimal exit.

This chapter highlights some of the most frequently encountered obstacles on the journey to Exit Readiness. For each, we'll explore its root causes and, more importantly, provide practical, EOS-aligned strategies to overcome it. Remember, every challenge you successfully navigate not only moves you closer to your exit goals but also builds a stronger, more resilient business in the present.

OBSTACLE 1: PERVASIVE OWNER DEPENDENCE

- **The Challenge:** The business heavily relies on the owner for key decisions, critical relationships (customers, suppliers), or essential operational knowledge. The owner is the bottleneck, and the business struggles to function effectively without their constant involvement.

- **Why It's a Problem for Exit Readiness:** Buyers are wary of businesses that are overly dependent on the seller. It signifies high risk, potential disruption post-acquisition, and a difficult integration. It significantly reduces valuation and transferability.

- **Solutions (Leveraging EOS & SxSE Principles)**

  - **Strengthen the People Component:** This is paramount. Get the Right People in the Right Seats on your Accountability Chart. Empower your leadership team to take full ownership of their roles and responsibilities.

  - **Delegate Relentlessly (and Effectively):** Use the "Let Go of the Vine" principle. Identify tasks and decisions the owner currently handles and systematically delegate them with clear expectations and support.

  - **Document Core Processes (Process Component):** Ensure critical operational knowledge is documented and institutionalized, not just residing in the owner's head. Make processes "Followed By All" (FBA).

  - **Build a Strong Leadership Team:** Invest in developing your leaders. They should be capable of running the day-to-day operations independently.

- **Systematically Transfer Key Relationships:**
  Gradually introduce other team members to key
  customer and supplier relationships. Make these
  relationships institutional, not personal to the owner.

- **Set Rocks for Owner Dependence Reduction:**
  Make reducing owner involvement in specific areas
  a quarterly Company Rock.

OBSTACLE 2: GAPS AND WEAKNESSES IN FINANCIAL REPORTING

- **The Challenge:** Financial statements are often late, inac-
  curate, or lack the detail and transparency that buyers
  expect. There might be inconsistent accounting practices
  or a failure to track key performance indicators (KPIs)
  that demonstrate value.

- **Why It's a Problem for Exit Readiness:** Unreliable
  financials erode buyer trust, make due diligence incredibly difficult and protracted, and can lead to significant
  valuation discounts or even deal collapse. Buyers need
  clean, credible numbers.

- **Solutions (Leveraging EOS & SxSE Principles)**

  - **Engage a Strong Financial Advisor/CFO:** Ensure
    you have the right financial leadership, whether
    internal or fractional. They should be responsible
    for the accuracy and timeliness of your financial
    reporting.

  - **Strengthen the Data Component:** Your Scorecard
    should include key financial KPIs. Ensure your
    accounting system is robust and your chart of
    accounts provides meaningful detail.

- ○ **Implement EOS Financial Disciplines:** This includes regular financial reviews, cash flow forecasting, and ensuring your numbers are discussed openly in Level 10 Meetings.

- ○ **Move Towards Accrual Accounting (If Applicable):** If you're on a cash basis, discuss with your financial advisor the benefits of moving to accrual accounting, which provides a more accurate picture of performance for most businesses.

- ○ **Consider a Quality of Earnings (QofE) Report Pre-Sale:** A QofE report, conducted by an independent accounting firm, can validate your financials and identify any issues before you go to market, increasing buyer confidence.

- ○ **Set Rocks for Financial System Improvement:** If there are known gaps, make addressing them a Company Rock (e.g., "Implement new accounting software," "Reduce financial statement closing time to 10 days").

OBSTACLE 3: WEAKNESSES IN THE MANAGEMENT TEAM

- • **The Challenge:** The leadership team may lack depth, experience in certain areas, or the ability to operate cohesively and strategically without the owner driving everything. There might be empty seats on The Accountability Chart or individuals who are not the Right People in the Right Seats (RPRS).

- • **Why It's a Problem for Exit Readiness:** A strong management team is one of the most valuable assets a buyer acquires. Weaknesses here signal operational risk and the need for the buyer to invest heavily in talent post-acquisition.

- **Solutions (Leveraging EOS & SxSE Principles)**

  - **Master the People Component:** This is non-negotiable. Use the People Analyzer to ensure you have RPRS in all leadership seats. Make tough people decisions where necessary.

  - **Invest in Leadership Development:** Provide training, coaching, and mentoring for your leaders. Help them grow into their roles and develop strategic thinking capabilities.

  - **Clearly Define Roles and Accountabilities (Accountability Chart):** Ensure every leader understands their five key roles and is held accountable for them.

  - **Foster a Healthy, Functional, Cohesive Leadership Team:** Use the EOS tools (Level 10 Meetings, IDS, V/TO) to build a team that communicates well, solves problems effectively, and is aligned on the Vision.

  - **Consider Strategic Hires or Advisor Support:** If there are critical skill gaps on the team (e.g., no strong sales leader, weak financial expertise), consider making a strategic hire or engaging a fractional expert/advisor to fill the void.

OBSTACLE 4: CHALLENGES WITH PROCESS DOCUMENTATION AND ADHERENCE

- **The Challenge:** Core business processes are not well-documented, or if they are, they are not consistently followed by all employees (FBA). This leads to inconsistencies, inefficiencies, and reliance on tribal knowledge.

- **Why It's a Problem for Exit Readiness:** Buyers want to see a business that can operate predictably and scalably. Lack of documented and followed processes indicates operational risk and makes it harder for them to understand how the business truly works.

- **Solutions (Leveraging EOS & SxSE Principles)**

  - **Commit to the Process Component:** Make documenting your 3–7 core processes a priority. Assign ownership for each process.

  - **Simplify Before You Document:** Don't just document what you currently do; look for ways to simplify and improve processes first.

  - **Use the "20/80" Approach to Documentation:** Focus on documenting the 20 percent of steps that deliver 80 percent of the results. Keep it practical and user-friendly.

  - **Train and Coach for Adherence (FBA):** Documentation is useless if it's not followed. Implement training programs and regular checks to ensure processes are being adhered to by everyone.

  - **Set Rocks for Process Improvement:** Make "Document and implement [Core Process X]" a regular feature in your quarterly Rocks until all key processes are covered.

OBSTACLE 5: CUSTOMER CONCENTRATION ISSUES

- **The Challenge:** A significant portion of the company's revenue comes from a very small number of customers (e.g., one customer represents 25+ percent of revenue).

- **Why It's a Problem for Exit Readiness:** This is a major red flag for buyers. The loss of a single large customer post-acquisition could cripple the business, making it a high-risk investment.

- **Solutions (Leveraging EOS & SxSE Principles)**

  - **Acknowledge and Track It (Data Component):** Add "Customer Concentration percentage (Top 3 Customers)" or similar to your Scorecard so it's visible weekly.

  - **Focus on Marketing and Sales (Vision Component & Process Component):** Implement strategies to acquire new customers and diversify your revenue base. Strengthen your sales process to consistently bring in new business.

  - **Deepen Relationships with Existing Key Customers:** While diversifying, also work to strengthen and institutionalize relationships with your current large customers. Ensure multiple touchpoints and strong contractual agreements if possible.

  - **Explore New Markets or Service Offerings:** Can you expand into new customer segments or offer additional services to your existing base to spread your revenue risk?

  - **Set Rocks for Customer Diversification:** Make "Reduce revenue from largest customer to X percent" or "Acquire Y new customers in Z segment" a Company Rock.

OBSTACLE 6: UNREALISTIC VALUATION EXPECTATIONS (VALUATION GAPS)

- **The Challenge:** The owner has an inflated idea of what their business is worth, often based on anecdotal evidence, emotion, or a misunderstanding of how businesses are valued in the M&A market.

- **Why It's a Problem for Exit Readiness:** Unrealistic expectations can lead to disappointment, a refusal to accept reasonable offers, or a failure to prepare adequately because the owner believes they are already "there."

- **Solutions (Leveraging EOS & SxSE Principles)**

  o **Engage an M&A Advisor Early:** Get a professional, market-based valuation range from an experienced M&A advisor well before you plan to sell. This provides a realistic baseline.

  o **Understand Value Drivers:** Work with your advisors to understand what truly drives value in your industry and for your type of business. Focus on improving those drivers.

  o **Focus on Profitability and Scalability:** These are often the biggest determinants of value. Use your EOS disciplines to improve both.

  o **Bridge the Gap with Value Creation:** If there's a gap between your desired valuation and the current market valuation, create a plan (with Rocks) to systematically close that gap by improving performance and addressing weaknesses.

OBSTACLE 7: OWNER'S EMOTIONAL UNREADINESS TO EXIT

- **The Challenge:** The owner is intellectually ready to sell but emotionally struggles with letting go of the business they've built, their identity as "the boss," or the daily routine and relationships.

- **Why It's a Problem for Exit Readiness:** Emotional unreadiness can lead to self-sabotage during the sale process, an inability to make clear decisions, or significant regret and dissatisfaction post-exit.

- **Solutions (Leveraging EOS & SxSE Principles)**

  o **Work with a Personal Coach (Six1 Framework):** This is specifically what they help with—navigating the personal and emotional aspects of major life transitions.

  o **Clarify Your "Life After Exit" Vision (Chapter 21):** Spend time defining what you want your next chapter to look like. Having a compelling future to move towards makes it easier to let go of the past.

  o **Gradually Reduce Involvement:** Start delegating more and stepping back from day-to-day operations well before a sale. This helps you and the business adjust.

  o **Develop Interests Outside the Business:** Cultivate hobbies, relationships, and activities that give you a sense of purpose and fulfillment beyond your company.

  o **Talk to Other Exited Entrepreneurs:** Hearing their experiences can provide perspective and reassurance.

EXIT-READY ACTIONS FOR OVERCOMING OBSTACLES

Proactively address potential roadblocks with these steps.

1. **Conduct an "Obstacle Brainstorm" with your leadership team.** Based on this chapter, which of these common obstacles are most likely to affect your journey? Add them to your Issues List.

2. **Prioritize the top 1–2 obstacles to address this quarter.** You can't fix everything at once. Choose the 1–2 obstacles that pose the biggest threat to your Exit Readiness and set Company Rocks to begin tackling them.

3. **Review your advisor team.** Do you have the right advisors in place (especially legal, financial, M&A, and potentially a coach) to help you navigate these challenges?

4. **Revisit your People Component.** Many obstacles (especially owner dependence and management team weaknesses) are rooted in people issues. Re-commit to getting RPRS in all seats.

5. **Focus on continuous improvement.** View obstacle-busting not as a one-time fix but as an ongoing part of strengthening your business through EOS.

Navigating the path to Exit Readiness will inevitably involve overcoming obstacles. By anticipating these common challenges and applying the disciplined, solution-oriented approach of EOS and the SxSE Model, you can turn these potential roadblocks into stepping stones towards building a more valuable, transferable, and ultimately, Exit-Ready company.

25

THE EXIT-READY LIFE

A chieving a state of Exit Readiness is not merely a business strategy; it profoundly impacts your life as an entrepreneur. It's about creating a business that serves your life, rather than a life consumed by your business. This final chapter before the conclusion explores the concept of "The Exit-Ready Life"—a way of operating and living that balances the demands of growing a successful EOS-run company with the strategic imperative of preparing for an eventual, optimal exit. It's about integrating the principles of Exit Readiness into your daily existence, finding purpose beyond your current enterprise, and thoughtfully preparing for the rich and fulfilling chapter that awaits you after you transition from your business.

Living an Exit-Ready Life means cultivating a mindset of stewardship, freedom, and foresight. It's about enjoying the fruits of your labor today, secure in the knowledge that you are building lasting value and have options for your future. It's the embodiment of running your business on EOS with an eye towards ultimate liberation and legacy, ensuring that both your professional and personal aspirations are aligned and achievable.

BALANCING BUSINESS GROWTH AND EXIT PREPARATION: A HARMONIOUS APPROACH

You have to walk away from all the things that don't fit.
The decision becomes as clear as someone asking you to eat
a worm. You'd say no with hesitation. Every decision can be
that easy. This applies to both your professional
and your personal life.

—Gino Wickman, Author of *Traction* & *Shine*, Creator of EOS®

Many entrepreneurs perceive a conflict between focusing on current business growth and preparing for a future exit. However, these two objectives are not mutually exclusive; in fact, they are highly synergistic when approached correctly. An Exit-Ready business, by its very nature, is a stronger, more scalable, and more profitable business. The disciplines you instill to make your company attractive to a buyer—strong leadership, clean financials, documented processes, reduced owner dependence—are the very same disciplines that drive sustainable growth and operational excellence today.

The key is to integrate Exit Readiness initiatives into your existing EOS framework. Your quarterly Rocks should include objectives that both fuel growth and enhance exit preparedness. For example, a Rock to expand into a new market (growth) can be coupled with a Rock to ensure the processes for that expansion are meticulously documented and transferable (Exit Readiness). The V/TO should reflect this dual focus, ensuring that your long-term vision encompasses both continued success and an optimal future transition.

LIVING THE EOS LIFE WHILE PREPARING FOR EXIT: DISCIPLINE AND FREEDOM

Running your company on EOS provides the perfect operating system for living an Exit-Ready Life. *The EOS Life*, as Gino Wickman describes it, is about doing what you love with people you love, making a huge difference, being compensated appropriately, and having time for other passions. Exit Readiness amplifies this. By systematically reducing your company's dependence on you, you gain more of that precious commodity: time. Time to think strategically, time to mentor your leadership team, time for your family, and time to pursue those "other passions."

The discipline of EOS—the Meeting Pulse, the Scorecard, Rocks, IDS—creates the structure that allows for this freedom. As you delegate more and empower your team through clear accountabilities (People Component) and robust systems (Process Component), you are not just building a sellable asset; you are crafting a more balanced and fulfilling life for yourself in the present.

FINDING PURPOSE BEYOND YOUR BUSINESS: ENVISIONING YOUR NEXT CHAPTER

A significant aspect of the Exit-Ready Life is proactively considering and cultivating your purpose beyond your current business. For many entrepreneurs, their identity is deeply intertwined with their company. Contemplating an exit can, therefore, raise questions about "what's next?" and "who will I be?"

It's crucial to start exploring these questions long before you actually sell. What other passions, interests, or causes do you want to dedicate your time and energy to? This could involve philanthropy, mentoring other entrepreneurs, starting a new venture (perhaps one with less operational intensity), dedicating more time to family, travel, or personal development. Your Personal Coach, a valuable member of your Six1 Framework, can be instrumental in helping you explore these avenues and define a compelling vision for your post-exit life. Having a clear sense of future purpose makes the prospect of exiting less daunting and more exciting.

CREATING A LEGACY THAT LASTS: MORE THAN JUST FINANCIAL WEALTH

Your legacy as an entrepreneur extends far beyond the financial wealth you accumulate. It encompasses the impact you've had on your employees, your customers, your community, and your industry. Living an Exit-Ready Life involves being intentional about this legacy. How do you want your business to be remembered? How can you ensure its positive impact continues even after you've moved on? This might influence your choice of exit strategy, perhaps favoring an ESOP or a sale to a buyer who shares your core values. It also involves how you steward your wealth. Will you establish a family foundation, support charitable causes, or invest in ventures that align with your values? Thinking about your legacy now, as part of your Exit Readiness journey, adds a profound layer of meaning to the process and helps shape decisions that will have a lasting impact.

PREPARING FOR LIFE AFTER EXIT

> *For most owners, the toughest part of exiting isn't the transaction—it's figuring out what comes next. Without a personal financial plan for life after the business, even a high-value sale can leave you feeling lost. That's why emotional clarity is just as critical as financial certainty.*
> —Steven A. Conte, President BRPG

Preparing for life after exit starts long before the deal closes. In the bonus chapter at the end of the book, you'll discover how Gino weaves ten disciplines into your daily rhythm—so you don't just leave your business in great hands, you step into your next chapter energized, clear-minded, and purpose-driven.

Read the bonus chapter and visit GinoWickman.com/shine to see how long-range thinking, boundary-setting, stillness, and the other disciplines become your personal roadmap for what comes next.

EXIT-READY ACTIONS: LIVING WITH INTENTION AND FORESIGHT

Embracing the Exit-Ready Life is an ongoing commitment to living and working with greater intention, balance, and foresight. Integrate these actions into your life, supported by your EOS disciplines.

1. **Integrate growth and Exit Goals.** Ensure your strategic planning (V/TO, quarterly Rocks) harmonizes objectives for business growth with initiatives that enhance Exit Readiness.

---

2. **Leverage EOS for personal freedom.** Actively use EOS tools and disciplines to reduce owner dependence, delegate effectively, and free up your time for strategic work and personal pursuits.

3. **Proactively explore your Post-Exit Purpose.** Dedicate time to reflect on and define what brings you meaning and fulfillment beyond your current business. Start cultivating those interests now.

4. **Be intentional about your legacy.** Consider the lasting impact you want to create. Let this inform your exit strategy and your plans for stewarding your wealth and influence.

5. **Utilize the Personal Readiness Planner.** Work through this tool to create a clear and actionable plan for your life after you transition from your business, addressing both practical and emotional aspects.

6. **Maintain open communication.** Regularly discuss your evolving thoughts on life, legacy, and future plans with your family, leadership team, and trusted Six1 Framework advisors.

7. **Embrace continuous learning and adaptation.** Just as your business evolves, so too will your personal vision. Stay open to new possibilities and be willing to adjust your plans for the Exit-Ready Life as you grow and learn.

Living an Exit-Ready Life is the ultimate expression of entrepreneurial success—building a thriving business that affords you freedom, security, and the opportunity to make a meaningful impact, both during your tenure and long after you've moved on to your next adventure. It's about designing a life and a business that truly serve your highest aspirations.

CONCLUSION:
YOUR EXIT-READY JOURNEY

You have now journeyed through the comprehensive framework of the Step-by-Step Exit (SxSE) system, a methodology meticulously designed to empower you, an EOS-driven entrepreneur, to transform your well-run business into one that is perpetually Exit-Ready. This book has aimed to demystify the process of exit preparation, illustrating how it seamlessly integrates with and extends the Entrepreneurial Operating System you already know and trust. The path to Exit Readiness is not merely about a transaction; it's a strategic imperative that enhances the value, resilience, and freedom your business provides, starting today.

From understanding the foundational SxSE Model and the collaborative power of the Six1 Framework, to navigating the emotional and practical aspects of the Exit-Ready Mindset and Vision, you've explored how to layer exit-focused thinking onto every component of your EOS implementation. We've delved into strengthening your team, data, issue resolution, processes, and traction, specifically to achieve an optimal exit. You've learned about the critical roles of your trusted advisors and the systematic steps to identify value gaps, implement strategic processes, protect and maximize value, and ultimately, extract that value effectively. Finally, we've considered the importance of managing your value post-exit and embracing the fulfilling prospects of an Exit-Ready Life.

RECAP OF KEY CONCEPTS: THE PILLARS OF SXSE

At its core, the SxSE system rests on several fundamental concepts.

1. **Exit Readiness is a continuous state, not a one-time event.** It's about building a business that is always prepared for a smooth and profitable transition, giving you maximum options and control.

2. **EOS provides a powerful foundation for Exit Readiness.** The discipline, clarity, and operational excellence fostered by EOS are invaluable prerequisites. SxSE builds upon this, adding the specific layers needed for a successful exit.

3. **Reducing owner dependence is paramount.** A business that can thrive without your daily involvement is inherently more valuable and transferable.

4. **A coordinated team of trusted advisors (the Six1 Framework) is essential.** Navigating the complexities of legal, financial, tax, M&A, wealth, and personal considerations requires expert guidance.

5. **Proactive planning and systematic execution are key.** Just as with EOS, achieving Exit Readiness requires setting clear goals (Rocks), assigning accountability, and maintaining a consistent rhythm.

THE CONTINUOUS NATURE OF EXIT READINESS: AN ONGOING DISCIPLINE

It is crucial to reiterate that achieving Exit Readiness is not a project with a finite end date prior to the actual exit itself. Rather, it is an ongoing discipline, a way of operating your business that should become as ingrained as your Level 10 Meetings or your quarterly Rock-setting sessions.

Market conditions change, your personal goals may evolve, and your business will continue to develop. Therefore, periodically revisiting your Exit Readiness Assessment, updating your Exit Vision, and refining your strategies with your Six1 Framework team are essential practices. This continuous improvement approach ensures that your business remains in an optimal state of preparedness, ready to capitalize on opportunities or navigate unforeseen circumstances with agility and confidence. The SxSE system is designed to be a living framework that adapts with you and your business over time.

NEXT STEPS FOR IMPLEMENTING SXSE: TURNING KNOWLEDGE INTO ACTION

Knowledge without action is merely potential. The true value of this book lies in its implementation. As you close these pages, consider the following immediate next steps to begin or accelerate your Exit-Ready journey.

1. **Conduct (or revisit) your Exit Readiness Assessment.** If you haven't already, use the Exit Readiness Assessment Tool (Chapter 22) to get an honest baseline of your current preparedness. If you've done it before, is it time for an update?

2. **Clarify your personal and business Exit Vision.** Dedicate time, perhaps with your spouse or key stakeholders, to refining your vision for your exit and your life beyond it. Integrate this into your V/TO.

3. **Assemble your initial Six1 Framework team.** Identify the key advisors you need to engage first. This often starts with your legal, financial, and potentially an M&A or exit planning specialist—schedule initial consultations.

4. **Set your first Exit Readiness Rocks.** Based on your assessment and vision, identify 1–3 critical Rocks for the next 90 days that will move you tangibly closer to Exit Readiness. Assign accountability and integrate them into your EOS Traction Component.

5. **Engage your leadership team.** Share your commitment to Exit Readiness with your leadership team. Educate them on the benefits and their crucial role in the process. Foster an open dialogue.

RESOURCES AVAILABLE TO SUPPORT YOUR JOURNEY: YOU ARE NOT ALONE

Embarking on the SxSE journey can be significantly enhanced by leveraging available resources. Beyond this book, consider seeking out Certified EOS Implementers who also have expertise in exit planning, or specialized exit planning advisors (like CEPAs) who understand the EOS framework. Peer groups and entrepreneurial forums can offer invaluable insights and shared experiences from others who are on, or have completed, similar journeys.

The official EOS Worldwide resources and the community of EOS-run companies also provide a wealth of knowledge and support. Remember, the SxSE system is designed to provide structure, but the journey is yours, and expert guidance can make it smoother and more effective.

FINAL THOUGHTS AND ENCOURAGEMENT: YOUR OPTIMAL FUTURE AWAITS

Building a business that runs effectively on EOS is a monumental achievement. Taking the further step to make that business truly Exit-Ready is the hallmark of a visionary entrepreneur who is not only a great operator but also a wise steward of value and a thoughtful architect of their own future. The path requires discipline, foresight, and a willingness to confront new challenges, but the rewards—in terms of financial return, personal freedom, peace of mind, and lasting legacy—are immense.

Your Exit-Ready journey is an investment in yourself, your family, your employees, and the future of the enterprise you've poured your heart into. Embrace the process with the same passion and commitment you brought to building your business. The principles and tools within the SxSE system, combined with the power of EOS, provide you with a clear and actionable roadmap. Trust the process, leverage your team, engage your advisors, and take consistent action. Your optimal exit and the fulfilling life that follows are within your reach. Now, go make it happen.

10 DISCIPLINES FOR MAXIMIZING YOUR ENERGY, IMPACT, AND INNER PEACE

BY GINO WICKMAN

I've added this chapter because I feel called to speak to you, the entrepreneur who has built something meaningful and is now preparing for what's next. You've spent years grinding, creating, leading, and growing. You've reached a level of success that most only dream about. Now you're thinking about the future, and possibly an exit. What you'll find in these next pages is not just information, but a system. A set of ten disciplines that will help you prepare your energy, your mind, and your life for the next stage.

These disciplines are designed for someone like you. You don't need motivation. You don't need a pep talk. You already show up. You've proven you can outwork, outlast, and outlead. You've taken care of your body, your mindset, and your team. That's a given. What you need now is a framework for turning the corner well. For using your energy with precision and intention as you move into your next chapter.

You're a racehorse. You've been running hard for a long time. But this next stretch isn't about running faster. It's about running smarter. It's about focusing your energy in a way that creates clarity, peace, and fulfillment...not just more results. The ten disciplines you're about to learn will help you stay sharp, avoid regret, and build a life beyond your business that's just as powerful as the one you built inside it.

Each discipline is simple. Each one is actionable. Each one works. At the end of every section, I'll ask you to take one specific action. I don't want you to just read, I want you to move. You've earned the right to live and lead from a deeper place. These ten disciplines will help you get there.

DISCIPLINE 1. 10-YEAR THINKING

This first discipline will literally transform your life. It transformed mine.

If you're like most driven human beings, you are preoccupied with today, this week, this month, maybe this year at the most. You want it now. This short-sightedness is limiting you.

Again, when you shift to long-range thinking, time will suddenly slow down. A peace will come over you. You will start to make better decisions. You will become more consistent. And the irony is that you will get to where you want to go faster.

When I learned this discipline at age thirty-five, it altered my life. As has been said many different ways, "People overestimate what they can accomplish in a year and underestimate what they can accomplish in ten years."

The reality is that you can accomplish anything in ten years.

Commit to the following three steps:

Step 1. Write the exact date ten years from now.
Step 2. Write the age you will be on that date.
Step 3. Take yourself there mentally, ten years from now, at that age.

Write down the number-one most important thing that you will want to have accomplished on that date. (You can write additional things that come to mind as well.)

You might have an income goal. It might be net worth. You might want to be completely free from your company. You might want to improve your physical health. There is no wrong answer. Yet for this discipline to be productive, you must write down a long-range goal.

Next, think about everything you have going on right now. All of your goals, plans, activities, and what is on your current to-do list. Do they all align with that ten-year goal? If not, you have some course correcting to do.

For example, when I was creating EOS, I decided that I wanted to have ten thousand companies running on EOS within the next two decades. When I set that goal, only fifty were running on EOS. I had no idea how to get to my goal number. But we have spent the last two decades making ten-year decisions, and I'm happy to say that we achieved my goal, almost to the day.

During every ten-year cycle, you will experience ups and downs. If you are always focused on the here and now, you will lose sight of the big picture. You will get caught up in the current growth spurt, downturn, or crisis. But, by taking a ten-year view, you'll see, in the grand scheme of things, that a downturn is merely a blip on the radar.

My business mentor, Sam Cupp, taught me what he called the "ten-year business cycle." He said, "Every ten years you're going to have two great years, six good years, and two terrible years that can put you out of business." His advice has held up since he shared it with me more than thirty years ago.

Whether a downturn is caused by a pandemic, a terrorist attack, a recession or depression, war, or general business ups and downs, you know it's coming. You can count on one every ten years for the rest of your life. The point is, don't be surprised by it. If you operate with a ten-year horizon, you will remain steadier and make better decisions.

The Great Recession of 2008–2009 was a blip in the grand scheme, although to most of us with businesses, it didn't feel that way at the time. The same goes for 9/11 and the dot-com crash. I can go all the way back in history. All of these seeming game-enders are blips.

The point is to be prepared. Knowing that a blip is going to come, you must have cash reserves. Always have six months of operating expenses in cash sitting in an account, both in your business and personal accounts, so you can endure six months of not bringing in any income.

10-Year Thinking is not so much about goal setting. You're reprogramming your brain to think in a longer time frame. You'll make better decisions, and you will get to your goals faster. Josh Holtzman experienced the amazing benefits of 10-Year Thinking when he owned and ran an IT services firm, American Data Company. When his company was generating $4 million in revenue, he set his eye on becoming a $40 million company in ten years. Yet when he set this target, he and his leadership team had no idea how they were going to reach it. But once they committed, the answers came.

Making ten-year decisions, the company joined forces with another player in their space. Unfortunately, they realized a few leadership team members weren't on board, so they replaced them with people who had greater experience and unflinching commitment. As you might imagine, they hit $40 million right at the ten-year mark. 10-Year Thinking will help you burn less energy, because you'll stop worrying about the short-term small stuff. And it will increase your total energy because you'll have a long-range vision to motivate you.

Again, when you go to bed at night, imagine—in vivid color—the most important ten-year goal in your mind. This will focus your thoughts and, if you believe in the law of attraction, increase the likelihood that you will achieve it.

DISCIPLINE 2. TAKE TIME OFF

You can't go, go, go all the time. You have to turn your brain off. As Stephen Covey said, "You have to 'sharpen the saw.'"

You have to rejuvenate and recharge your batteries. You must work hard *and* play hard.

Please don't confuse the discipline of unplugging from work, turning your brain off, and restoring your energy with the vital importance of working hard when you are working. It's just that you also need to take time off to reset.

I take 150 days off per year (which includes most weekends). I've done it for over twenty years, and I'm convinced I'm further ahead because of it. I get more done, have more energy, and am more creative with better ideas.

When you unplug and then come back to the business, you view problems differently. You see them better. You see them clearer. As the old adage teaches us, "When I go slow, I go fast."

Entrepreneurs often push back by saying, "I can't take time off," "I don't like to take time off," or "That's not how I work." Some people just don't know how to turn it off. They're incapable of taking a break. They *need* to work. They feel like they're supposed to be working.

Please understand that they have a disorder. They are workaholics. (Rule of thumb: Any word with "-aholic" at the end is a disease and undesirable.) When you stop the grindstone, the healing begins. Just like during sleep, when you get the required one to two hours of "deep sleep"—the most restorative and rejuvenating stage—that's when your brainwaves, heartbeat, and breathing slow down. Your blood pressure drops and your muscles relax. This stage of sleep improves memory and learning and produces growth hormones. Your energy is replenished, your cells are regenerated, and your immune system is strengthened. All because you stopped and slept.

Imagine if you didn't sleep (or get enough deep sleep). It's the same as working all the time. You deprive yourself of the many benefits going on under the surface that you can't see until you take a break from work.

Decide on the number of days off you will take per year. Commit to that figure in writing. Here's the simple math: If you're taking every weekend off, you're already taking 104 days off. Now add in your vacations and you'll have your number.

Please write your "days off" commitment right now.

DISCIPLINE 3. KNOW THYSELF

This discipline helps you *be* yourself more than *know* yourself. But you can't be yourself until you first know thyself.

To start, you need to be comfortable and ready to let your freak flag fly, which simply means you being fully, unapologetically you. When we are fully ourselves, we appear quirky to others. The fact is that the world wants to judge us, and that squashes our light. The sooner you decide to be yourself 100 percent of the time, the sooner you'll have more energy. Because you won't have to fake it anymore. Being something you are not consumes a lot of energy. As the saying goes, "Hell on earth would be meeting the person you could have been."

Knowing thyself is a matter of understanding your strengths, weaknesses, personality, and M.O. There are many different approaches to knowing thyself. You can use profiling tools like DiSC, Myers-Briggs, Culture Index, or Kolbe. I've taken at least ten of them, and they've all had an impact on my clarity.

Another way to know yourself better is to get therapy. I've never met anyone who didn't need a little bit. I did in my twenties, and I'm grateful for what I learned.

Randy McDougal, a successful entrepreneur, shares his experience with therapy: "For me, therapy has given me the freedom to be vulnerable and curious about life and relational difficulties. It has made me comfortable being me, instead of feeling like I have to prove to those around me that I'm 'okay.'

"Through therapy, I've learned to separate my value as a person from what I do or do not do. I learned how in early life I developed 'compensations' to help me get through challenges. While most of my compensations are socially acceptable (working hard, keeping busy, making money), they are distractions and they can undermine me and those closest to me."

Randy also offers this advice: "Many people try one therapist and then give up. All therapists are not the same, and we each need to find the one who fits us and where we are in life right now."

Another way to know thyself is to get honest feedback from the people in your life. Ask them what they see as your strengths and weaknesses. Ask them what you do well and where you could improve.

In addition to operating in your personal sweet spot, which maximizes your skills and abilities, knowing thyself is fully being you 100 percent of the time. You fully express your personality, living by your M.O., acknowledging your weaknesses, and capitalizing on your strengths.

For example, learning and embracing that I was an introvert was incredibly freeing. I have never loved small talk and social gatherings, and I thought there was something wrong with me. Instead, I was just being the introvert I am, and knowing that was liberating.

The more you know yourself and live that way, the better you will function. You'll stop feeling apologetic for being who you are. You won't waste energy trying to be someone you think you're supposed to be. Have you ever felt you are one person at work, one person at home, one person out with your friends, and so on? You're trying to be all things to all people.

The textbook example of this happened when my wife threw me a surprise thirtieth birthday party. When I saw a hundred people yell, "Surprise!" I was first excited, then struck by a sinking feeling of "Holy shit! Who am I going to be today?"

That's because I could see six different factions of my life in one room.

There were my employees and business partners. My family—mom, dad, brothers, and cousins. My wife's family. My high school friends. My entrepreneur friends and friends from the neighborhood.

I realized I was literally a different person with each of these six groups of people. With my employees, I was "boss Gino." With my high school friends, I was "crazy Gino." With my new friends, I was "less-crazy Gino." And so on.

It was a wake-up call, and from that day o,n I was "authentic Gino."

Imagine the energy I was expending being who I felt I had to be with each individual group.

Now I am simply myself with everyone. I am hardworking, hard-playing, passionate, intense, beer-drinking, obsessive, introverted, gritty me. And being that way makes me feel a thousand pounds lighter.

Being someone you are not saps your energy.

So, who are you?

Please commit to one step you will take in the next week to move closer to knowing thyself. Maybe take Kolbe or one of the other profiling tools. Schedule a session with a therapist. Reach out to a friend, a family member, or a peer, and ask, "What are my three greatest strengths and my three greatest weaknesses?"

DISCIPLINE 4. BE STILL

Whether you meditate, pray, contemplate, or journal, spend ten to thirty minutes every day in silence. Being still will be transformative.

As an entrepreneur, you go hard all day, every day. But at intervals, you must stop. Literally put on the brakes and just breathe.

I have been amazed at how closing my eyes and breathing shifts me out of my head and into my body. It centers me. It grounds me. It helps create absolute clarity on the project I'm working on or the problem I'm trying to solve.

Someone taught it to me this way. Imagine a glass jar full of water and a little bit of sand. Imagine shaking that jar. The water would be cloudy, murky, and unclear—like most of us when we go, go, go all day, every day. But if you let the glass jar sit for a few minutes, the sand settles and the water becomes clear, lucid, and calm. Just like what will happen to you if you are still for a few minutes.

This discipline will increase and focus your energy. You will feel like you just drank a cup of coffee, but without the jitters or the caffeine crash sixty minutes later. Rob Dubé, co-owner of imageOne, an $18 million managed-print-solutions and software company with fifty employees, illustrates the power of this discipline with his own story. One day, he was on vacation with his family in northern Michigan just after selling their company (which they later bought back). It was a beautiful day, but he was inside his home working, feeling stressed, anxious, and out of control. He had recently read an article about mindfulness and meditation, so he decided to try it.

He chose a chair in one corner and sat in silence. The calm he achieved had such a profound impact on him that he made it a regular practice. This discipline led him to write a book titled *donothing: The most rewarding leadership challenge you will ever take,* in which he teaches leaders the practice of being still. He also offers an annual silent retreat for those leaders who want to take this discipline to a deeper level.

Tomorrow morning, before you start your day, take at least ten minutes. Sit quietly in a chair. Be still. Pause and breathe. See what happens. Do this for thirty days and see for yourself. It will have an incredible impact on your energy, your mood, and your relationships.

DISCIPLINE 5. KNOW YOUR 100%

You should know the exact amount of time you will devote to your work if you want to maximize your energy. This is known as your "work container," which you must protect. What makes this discipline different is that it also works in the context of managing your energy. You need to protect your energy. Deciding your perfect number of working hours will determine your peak energy. It's when literally one more hour of work would be less fun or start burning you out.

Think about your work M.O.: your ideal time to wake up and what time you prefer to get home, along with how many days a week you want to work and how many weeks per year. This discipline, when followed religiously, maintains your high energy.

To illustrate, Meg Mayhugh runs her own consulting firm and has been on the leadership team as the head of HR and head of growth for several companies. She lives by this discipline and is extraordinary about helping people understand the concept of leveraging their time, both in her coaching and by her example. She is a single parent of three kids and works hard to be disciplined about both protecting her 100% and asking for and finding assistance. She delegates tasks unapologetically so that she can be a hockey coach, a volunteer board member at a local nonprofit, and a lifeguard. Juggling her tasks is not always easy, but she makes it look that way.

Personally, I now work forty weeks per year and forty hours per week (I worked fifty-five hours a week for over thirty years). That is my perfect formula to maximize my energy.

If you don't protect your container, where does work end? If work hours are negotiable, then you'll always operate above your 100 percent, and you'll get burned out. You won't be the best version of yourself.

Write down your 100 percent, both the number of hours per week and the number of weeks per year.

DISCIPLINE 6. SAY NO . . . OFTEN

With the first five disciplines in place, this discipline becomes easy. Your long-range plans are now clear, your time commitments are now clear, you know who you are, and you are taking time to be still every day. With this clarity, it becomes obvious what you should not be doing and saying no to.

In *Essentialism*, a great book on the subject of simplifying your life, author Greg McKeown addresses the necessity of saying no. He states, "The very thought of saying no literally brings us physical discomfort. We feel guilty." He goes on to say, "Either we can say no and regret it for a few minutes or we can say yes and regret it for days, weeks, months, or even years."

McKeown also shares a great principle on how you should filter your decisions: "If it isn't a hell yes, then it's a no."

You have to walk away from all the things that don't fit. The decision becomes as clear as someone asking you to eat a worm. You'd say no without hesitation. Every decision can be that easy. This applies to both your professional *and* your personal life.

You will reduce the guilt you feel by saying no because now your reason for saying no is so obvious. You will discontinue doing the things you shouldn't be doing. You'll no longer get sucked into doing things that drain your energy like they used to, when you would say yes.

Please write down one thing you've recently agreed to do when you should have said no. It might be an appointment that you scheduled, a project you committed to doing, or an event that you planned. And then commit to saying no to at least one person this week.

DISCIPLINE 7. DON'T DO $25-AN-HOUR WORK (IF YOU WANT TO EARN SIX FIGURES)

I'm not knocking $25-an-hour work, and I'm not knocking people who make $25 an hour. We need people making $25, because that makes the economy work. If you are happy making $25 an hour, amen and hallelujah! But I'm assuming the reader of this book is either making six figures or more or wants to make six figures or more. If my assumptions are correct, then you shouldn't be doing $25-an-hour work.

You must eliminate all administrative tasks from your life. You shouldn't be checking emails, opening mail, managing your calendar, scheduling appointments, booking travel, or doing follow-up and follow-through work. Those things drain your energy. You must delegate them all.

Let's take checking your own email, for example. I dread checking and responding to email; it distracts me and saps my energy. As a result, I have not read or answered my daily email in more than fifteen years. My solution was simple: I hired an administrative assistant to do it. Every day, I am free to do my craft and not get bogged down. Get an assistant to do your administrative tasks so you can spend all of your time in your personal sweet spot, which provides you with energy.

For example, the Visionary entrepreneur of a fast-growing international shipping company was still reviewing and approving every invoice before it went out. His executive assistant walked into his office late one night as he was poring over the invoices and asked, "Why are you doing that?"

The Visionary responded, "Because I'm the owner."

His assistant said, "It takes you two hours a day, it makes you upset, and honestly, you are not very good at it. Let me do it."

They put a process in place where she would approve anything under $50,000, and he would approve anything above. This freed up almost 10 hours a week for the Visionary to focus on growing the company.

Please write a list of all of the administrative tasks you are doing. You've just written a job description for your new assistant. Now, go hire one. You might only need someone for 10 hours a week or 30 hours a week, maybe full-time. But that person is out there waiting to take those burdens off you. Because that is what gives *them* energy.

DISCIPLINE 8. PREPARE EVERY NIGHT

I've been practicing this discipline for 25 years. You should go to bed knowing exactly what you're going to do tomorrow. You have to hit the ground running when you wake up. This powerful discipline was taught to me by my mentor, Sam Cupp.

Every night before I go to bed, I lay out my entire next day on a legal pad. I use a legal pad because I believe in the power of writing by hand. I time-block everything I need to do: the calls I need to make, the meetings I need to attend, the projects

I need to finish. I list them all in chronological order so that my day is already charted.

If you do this, you will sleep better. You will wake up with ideas and be more creative. You'll wake up with answers to problems and projects you need to work on the next day. That's because your subconscious will be working on them during the night while you sleep.

If you are the kind of person who says, "I like to be spontaneous and let the day come at me when I wake up," or "I like to check my emails first and see what's in store for me today," or "I just react to the calls and problems that come at me in the morning," then you have lost control of your life. You're letting other people manage your energy.

Please do this before you go to bed tonight: lay out the next day. You can do it on a legal pad or on a tablet, in your calendar, in a planner, or on any device you prefer. Carry out this practice for an entire week, and decide for yourself if it works. I get such great feedback when people first try this discipline. You'll see right away how much it helps.

DISCIPLINE 9. PUT EVERYTHING IN ONE PLACE

Let's take an idea from the last discipline one step further. I've been working from a legal pad for thirty years. My clients, friends, and peers lovingly laugh at my legal pad because it seems so archaic. It's always with me: when I walk into any meeting, when I'm on a call, when I'm driving. I live from a legal pad.

You can execute this discipline on any technology. It doesn't have to be a legal pad. Oddly, if I advocated using a tablet, many people would probably take me more seriously. But I recommend paper. As I've mentioned, I believe in the science behind the power of writing by hand. When you write things down that way, you retain them better.

Here's the typical day of an entrepreneur. Let's assume you started working from the list you laid out the night before. As you work through the day, you have meetings and phone calls, you'll get ideas, you make commitments and promises to people, and you have to remember many work items. Normally, you put each of these to-do items somewhere, maybe on a sticky note, and set it aside. You might try to remember all of them in your head. You might tap them into your phone or text them to yourself. Yet by the end of the day, you have compiled a mess of stuff you're supposed to do. And the truth of the matter is, you've probably forgotten some of it, and you're about to let people down. Your brain can't keep track of all of that stuff.

At this point, I'm sure I don't have to tell you what that is doing to your energy. I'm guessing you lost a little energy just reading that paragraph.

In this discipline, you will put all of those items in one place. You first have to decide what that one place is. Your equivalent of a legal pad.

When I make somebody a promise, have an idea, need to remember something, or have to follow up on a task, I write it down on my ever-present legal pad. I capture it there so that at the end of the day, I can pull all of those commitments and ideas off the pad and put them on the list for the next day. Or, I might take care of some things right then and there at night while I'm preparing. I might compartmentalize others as to-dos in my calendar or time-block them as a project to work on two weeks from now.

The point is that you can organize all of those things at the end of the day when you have everything right in front of you. Also, by quickly writing all of the things that come at you throughout the day, you can concentrate on the task at hand and not get distracted.

Please try this tomorrow. Decide the one place you're going to put every single workday commitment, idea, and thought. Then capture everything that comes up throughout the day in that place. Try it for a week and see how it affects your productivity and energy.

DISCIPLINE 10. BE HUMBLE

What does being humble have to do with managing your energy? Everything! Let me explain. First of all, I'm not talking about being weak. Humble people are powerful and strong. Pastor and author Rick Warren said, "Humility is not thinking less of yourself, it is thinking of yourself less."

Start by picturing a spectrum. On one end is "arrogant." On the other is "humble." I'm guessing you know both types of people.

The definition of humble is, ironically, "your estimate of your own importance in comparison to others," and the definition of arrogant is "the way you view your level of importance in comparison to others." They are both saying the same thing.

What is your view of yourself? How do you view your level of importance in comparison to others? Simply put, humble people don't feel they are more important than anyone else. And arrogant people feel that they are.

To see how you stack up, draw the spectrum, and then put a hash mark where you feel you are on it. If you want a more accurate depiction, ask someone close to you where they would put you on the spectrum.

Whether you are arrogant or humble, of course, you can be extremely successful. There are thousands of examples of both types of people. What I have discovered, however, is that the journey of life is better if you are humble. There is a universal law—the boomerang, karma, whatever you call it—that being humble in life attracts more humble people to you, which leads to more happiness, friends, and people who want to fight for you and be with you.

I am grateful for my father-in-law, Neil Pardun, for teaching me humility. When I was in my twenties, I was going down a path of arrogance. He altered the course of my life by his example.

He didn't even know he did it. He didn't pull me aside and say, "Hey, be more humble." He showed it through the power of his actions.

Neil was a wealthy man who made his money constructing industrial buildings and who also owned a golf course. He was a tough guy, down-to-earth, authentic, and generous. He was always fully himself and didn't care what anyone thought. He treated everyone the same and always made you feel important. He was liked and respected by everyone.

I have two favorite stories about him. Once, while I was driving him home, he saw a set of ratty, dusty, used, thirty-year-old golf clubs in someone's trash on garbage day. He yelled, "Stop the car!" He jumped out and garbage-picked the tattered old clubs because they could be used at his golf course. It was not beneath him to pick someone's trash for something he thought was valuable.

The second story happened while he was working at the golf course. He would cut the greens every day while wearing his old jeans and a T-shirt. One day, some young kids were horsing around on the course while he was on his mower. He rode over and asked them to stop. They asked, "Who do you think you are, old man?"

Neil said, "I'm the owner."

One of the kids said, "Yeah, right!"

You'd never guess he had money. I'm thankful every day that Neil was in my life. In terms of energy management, when you are humble, you get more energy back from people than you put out. You also attract more people who mirror your attitude. Do you want to be surrounded by humble people or arrogant people?

Please list the five most important people in your life. Then reach out to each and ask them where they would place you on the arrogant–humble spectrum. This will help you determine how you are showing up in the world.

So, here they are, the 10 Disciplines for Managing & Maximizing Your Energy.

1. 10-Year Thinking
2. Take Time Off
3. Know Thyself
4. Be Still
5. Know Your 100%
6. Say No . . . Often
7. Don't Do $25-an-Hour Work
8. Prepare Every Night
9. Put Everything in One Place
10. Be Humble

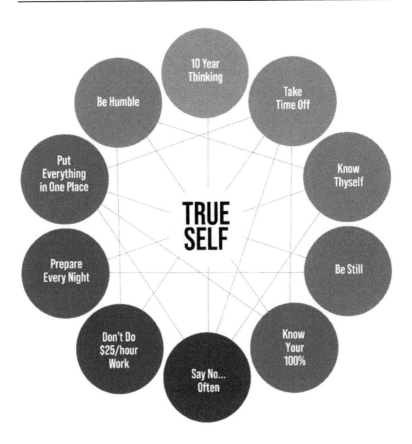

Each discipline is easy to understand. Doing them is harder. Please don't underestimate them, as they will have a profound impact on your life.

If you do every one of these disciplines to maximize your energy, impact, and inner peace, you will be a force of nature.

We believe in something deeper than outer success. We believe in the power of becoming your True Self and doing it alongside others. At The 10 Disciplines, we're building a community of like-minded leaders through continued education and programs designed to help driven people go deeper and farther. There are two main ways to get involved: You can learn more about the 10 Disciplines and our deep dive in our book *Shine* by visiting the10disciplines.com/book, or you can enjoy our Shed and Shine podcast at the10disciplines.com/podcast. We're always here to help support you on your journey.

WORKSHEET

What actions can you take in the next seven days to help you manage and maximize your energy?

_____

_____

_____

_____

_____

_____

_____

_____

_____

_____

_____

_____

_____

_____

_____

_____

_____

_____

ABOUT THE AUTHORS

TYLER SMITH

Tyler was one of Gino Wickman's first clients and has spent over 25 years as a hands-on entrepreneur. He led the build-and-exit of Niche Retail (chronicled in Traction®), served for over 10 years guiding EOS's technology and marketing efforts—including creating Base Camp and EOS ONE—and today coaches companies as an EOS Implementer. Tyler serves as Step by Step Exit's Visionary and EOS Implementer.

KELLY J. CARTER

Kelly is the co-founder and CEO of Beacon Retirement Planning Group, bringing over 35 years of experience as a financial life planner focused on helping entrepreneurs align their personal goals with smart wealth and tax strategies while preparing for successful transitions. As a Certified Exit Planning Advisor, Kelly works closely with EOS Implementers to guide their clients through the Step-by-Step Exit process—identifying the value gap, addressing key financial, legal, and operational challenges, and positioning the company to be truly exit-ready. He also serves as the Integrator for Step by Step Exit.

Get a **valuation** of your business, identify the **gaps** that are affecting it's value

This report will show you:
- What your business is worth
- Risk mitigation and growth opportunities
- Value Acceleration Strategies

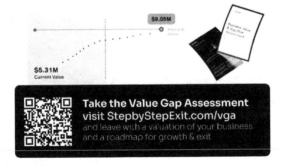

Take the Value Gap Assessment
visit StepbyStepExit.com/vga
and leave with a valuation of your business
and a roadmap for growth & exit

YOU CAN BE DRIVEN AND HAVE PEACE

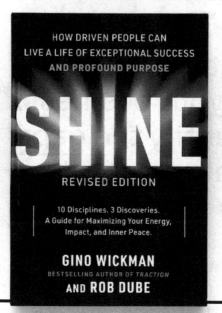

HOW DRIVEN PEOPLE CAN
LIVE A LIFE OF EXCEPTIONAL SUCCESS
AND PROFOUND PURPOSE

SHINE

REVISED EDITION

10 Disciplines. 3 Discoveries.
A Guide for Maximizing Your Energy,
Impact, and Inner Peace.

GINO WICKMAN
BESTSELLING AUTHOR OF *TRACTION*
AND ROB DUBE

GET A GRIP ON YOUR BUSINESS

WITH THE
ENTREPRENEURIAL
OPERATING SYSTEM®

EOSWorldWide.com